101 DISEASES
YOU DON'T WANT TO GET

MICHAEL POWELL WITH DR. OLIVER FISCHER

THUNDER'S MOUTH PRESS
NEW YORK

Published by
Thunder's Mouth Press
An imprint of Avalon Publishing Group Inc.
245 West 17th St., 11th Floor
New York, NY 10011

AVALON
publishing group incorporated

Copyright © 2005 by Gusto Company AS

First printing September 2005

Published in the UK in 2005 by Cassell Illustrated
A division of Octopus Publishing Group limited
2-4 Heron Quays
London E14 4JP

Publisher's note: The views expressed herein are the personal views of the author and are not intended to reflect the views of the publisher. The information contained herein is for entertainment purposes only and should not replace a professional diagnosis by a healthcare professional. The drugs and medicines mentioned in this book are the property of their respective proprietors.

Written by Michael Powell with Dr. Oliver Fischer
Illustrations and Photography: Custom Medical Stock Photo Inc
Executive Editors Gusto Company: James Tavendale and Ernesto Gremese
Edited by Stephen Lynn
Layout and typesetting by Ghislain Viau
Art Direction by Saroyan Humphrey and Magnus Rakeng

All rights reserved. No part of this publication may be reproduced or transmitted in any form or by any means, electronic or mechanical, including photocopy, recording, or any information storage and retrieval system now known or to be invented, without permission in writing from the publisher, except by a reviewer who wishes to quote brief passages in connection with a review written for inclusion in a magazine, newspaper, or broadcast.

Library of Congress Control Number is avalable: 2005927281

ISBN 1-56025-737-7

9 8 7 6 5 4 3 2 1

Printed in China
Distributed by Publishers Group West

TABLE OF CONTENTS

101 DISEASES
YOU DON'T WANT TO GET

MICHAEL POWELL WITH DR. OLIVER FISCHER

Nobody likes being sick, but we are happy to read about illness safe in the knowledge that we'd have to travel thousand of miles from home even to be exposed to some of the diseases in this world, let alone catch them.

But that doesn't mean that you're not a little curious about what would happen if you did, right? Besides, one day you might be on the receiving end of one of these nasties, especially since global warming is hastening climate change at an unprecedented rate.

So here's the lowdown on over 100 of the most virulent and deadly diseases on the planet (and quite possibly in the universe). From STDs to retroviruses, if they can kill, disfigure or irreparably damage your internal organs, you'll find them here.

This book should not be used as a substitute for visiting a physician. Its purpose is to satisfy your curiosity rather than as a diagnostic tool, and it is in no way an alternative to visiting a trained doctor, changing behind a screen and being rewarded with an expert opinion and a prescription. So, the moment you suspect you've picked up a dose of something unmentionable or start coughing up worms, get yourself off to your health centre and, by all means, take this book to keep you amused in the waiting room.

At first glance the prolific parasites, bacterial bad news and viral visitations that spill off every page might make you scared to leave the safety of your bedroom, but be reassured that sometimes even the worst case of agoraphobia won't save you from that infinitesimal chance.

That's a humbling thought when you consider that on the other side of the world, over 10 million children under five years of age die each year as a result of common, treatable infections such as pneumonia, chronic diarrhea and malaria. The price of this book could prevent the deaths of several of them. So while you 'oooh' and 'aaaah' your way through this voyeuristic compendium, be mindful of those for whom experience is their greatest teacher.

ACROMEGALY

What is it?
A condition caused by abnormally high levels of growth hormones in the body.

Where can I catch it?
Growth hormone production becomes too high as a result of a tumor, most often in the pituitary gland.

Major outbreaks
Acromegaly is a very rare condition, affecting four in every one million men and women annually in the United States, most commonly between the ages of 40 and 45.

How do I know I have it?
The disease progresses so slowly that it is often quite advanced before people realise they have it. The first symptoms you will notice are that your rings and shoes are becoming too small; your hands and feet are growing larger. Your jaw, forehead and the side of your face may also grow larger, making your facial appearance different. Again, these changes happen so slowly that they may go undetected. You may experience arthritic pain and back pain as the cartilage in your joints and back grows larger. You may find it more difficult to breathe during sleep, leading to tiredness by day. Your skin texture will change, becoming oily and thick; you may even develop acne. Your fingers and toes may tingle as your growing bones trap nerves. You may sweat more, and have lots of skin tags. Your teeth and jaw line will change so that you will notice a change in your bite. You may experience partial or complete loss of vision and headaches.

Chances of survival
Acromegaly is not fatal, but it can lead to other complications if left untreated, such as heart problems, high blood pressure and diabetes, and these complications can be fatal.

How do I get rid of it?
In most cases, you will undergo surgery to remove the tumor(s) in your pituitary gland, after which you will be given drugs that aim to bring your hormone productions back down to normal levels. Where surgery and drugs do not cure the tumor, you may then require radiation therapy, often over a period of several years.

AFRICAN TRYPANOSOMIASIS
(Sleeping Sickness)

What is it?
A parasitic disease. The parasites, *Trypanosoma*, are single-celled microscopic organisms called protozoa that are transmitted to humans by blood-sucking tsetse flies. Tsetse flies live in Africa, and are found in vegetation by rivers and lakes, forests and wooded savannah.

Where can I catch it?
It occurs only in parts of sub-Saharan Africa where tsetse flies are endemic. There are epidemics in Angola, Democratic Republic of Congo and Sudan, and it is highly endemic in Cameroon, Central African Republic, Chad, Congo, Côte d'Ivoire, Guinea, Mozambique, Uganda and United Republic of Tanzania.

Major outbreaks
There have been three serious epidemics in Africa over the last century: one between 1896 and 1906, mostly in Uganda and the Congo Basin, one in 1920 in several African countries and one that began in 1970 and is still in progress.

Almost 45,000 cases were reported in 1999, but the World Health Organization (WHO) estimates that the number of people affected is 10 times greater.

How do I know I have it?
In the early phase you'll experience fever, headaches, pains in the joints and itching. In the second or neurological phase, the parasite infests the central nervous system causing confusion, sensory disturbances and poor co-ordination and disturbance of the sleep cycle.

Chances of survival
Without treatment, nil. With early detection, your chances are good. If you don't receive treatment before the second phase, you will suffer irreversible neurological damage.

How do I get rid of it?
If you receive treatment early enough, your chances of recovery are high. During the first phase, you will be treated with Suramine and Pentamidine. In the second phase, expect to be given an arsenic derivative called Melarsoprol which is, at present, the only drug available on the market to treat the advanced stage of the disease, but it has nasty neurological side effects.

ALVEOLAR ECHINOCOCCOSIS (AE)

What is it?
A tumor-like infection caused by infestation with the larval stage of a microscopic tapeworm, *Echinococcus multilocularis*, found in foxes, coyotes, sheep, dogs and cats. Human infection is rare but potentially fatal.

Where can I catch it?
The eggs of the tapeworm are found in the fecal matter of infected animals. If you accidentally swallow these eggs you will become infected. They may either get on your hands after petting your dog or cat, then are transferred to your mouth, or they may be on fruit, berries, greens or herbs collected outdoors and improperly washed.

Major outbreaks
It is found worldwide, but mostly in the Northern Hemisphere. Cases have been recorded in central Europe, Russia, China, central Asia, Japan and the north central region of North America.

How do I know I have it?
The tumor-like larval mass usually grows in the liver over many years, without causing any symptoms. When symptoms do appear, they usually resemble those of liver cancer, including pain below the ribs, weakness and weight loss, although tumors may also grow in other organs such as the brain or lungs.

Chances of survival
Without treatment AE can be fatal, either because the cysts compromise vital organs or because, if they burst, they spread the organism throughout your body and send you into anaphylactic shock.

How do I get rid of it?
A scolicide is injected into the cyst to kill the larvae, and then surgery is performed to remove the masses. This is followed by several weeks of medication (benzimidazoles, mainly albendazole) to prevent re-growth.

What is it?
An intestinal parasitic infection of either *Ancylostoma duodenale* or *Necator americanus*, roundworms that grow to 13mm (½ in) in length. Also known as hookworm.

Where can I catch it?
Ancylostoma duodenale is common in northern Africa, northern Asia, southern Europe and parts of South America. Hookworm infections caused by *Necator americanus* occasionally occur in the southeastern United States. Eggs released into the soil in feces will hatch into larvae that can burrow through your skin if you walk barefoot. From here they are carried in your bloodstream to the lungs, where they travel through the respiratory tract into the back of your mouth and are swallowed. Once in the small intestine, they fix onto the intestinal wall and begin feeding on your blood. *Ancylostoma Duodenale* lives for up to a year, *Necator americanus* for up to five years, during which time the females produce up to 25,000 eggs every day, which will pass in your stools.

Major outbreaks
Infections of *Necator americanus* have been largely controlled since the early 20th century so that hookworm infection

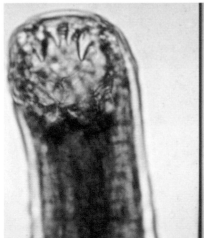

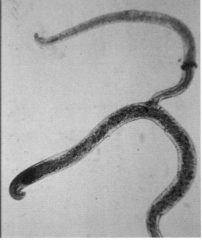

in the United States is now rare. In tropical areas worldwide, Ancylostomiasis infections can be as high as 80 percent of the population, and it is estimated that a quarter of the world's population have the infection at any one time.

How do I know I have it?

Your skin around the area where the larvae first penetrate will begin to itch, and a rash will appear, known as 'ground itch'. You may develop a mild fever and a cough as the worms work their way through your lungs, which in some cases might develop into wheezing. Your abdomen may become tender, and you may also develop anemia as your iron levels drop, which leaves you feeling tired, listless and pale. The anemia can trigger an abnormally fast heartbeat (tachycardia), and you may develop a limp.

Chances of survival

If treated, Ancylostomiasis is not life threatening and is easily cured. However, children who are chronically infected, over a long period of time and by many worms, can develop anemia to such an extent that their mental and physical growth is stunted, sometimes permanently. It can cause an enlargement of the heart and can be fatal, especially in the very young.

How do I get rid of it?

You will be given a anti-parasitic drug: mebendazole, albendazole or pyrantel. If you have also developed hookworm anemia, you will also be given iron supplements and will be recommended a high-protein diet.

What is it?

Angiostrongylus is a parasitic roundworm that infects rats. Two forms, *A. cantonensis* and *A. costaricensis*, can infect humans.

Where can I catch it?

Snails and slugs may eat rat feces that is infected with the immature larval form of the worm. Fortunately the parasites can only mature in rats, so while humans aren't part of the parasitic lifecycle, they can become infected by eating the snails (and possibly from slug and snail trails left on food such as salad). It can't be 'caught' from other people.

Major outbreaks

Most of the known infections were in Southeast Asia and the Pacific Islands, although there have been a few cases in the Caribbean. In 1993 a boy in the United States became infected after eating a snail for a dare.

How do I know I have it?

Some people have no symptoms or very mild ones that clear up quickly. If *A. cantonensis* larvae enter the brain they can cause a rare type of meningitis (eosinophilic meningitis), which causes a headache, stiff neck, fever and vomiting and a tingling sensation on the skin.

Chances of survival

There have been fatalities, but even if you develop meningitis your chances of recovery are excellent.

How do I get rid of it?

There is no cure, only palliative care for the painful symptoms. The parasites will soon die without treatment, but the symptoms may last for weeks, even months. If you develop eosinophilic meningitis you may be given antibiotics, but it should be fought off by your body's immune system even without drugs.

ANISAKIASIS

What is it?
A parasitic infection caused by swallowing larvae of the roundworms *Anisakis simplex* and *Pseudoterranova decipiens*.

Where can I catch it?
Adult stages of the parasite live in the stomach of marine mammals. Eggs are passed in their feces, hatch into larvae in the water and swim around until they are swallowed by crustaceans, where they develop into third-stage larvae, which then infect fish and squid. Humans (and marine mammals) become infected by eating these fish raw or undercooked.

Major outbreaks
The parasite is found worldwide, but human infection is greatest in cultures where eating fish is widespread. The first case was described in 1876, and there were many cases in the Netherlands in the 1950s and 1960s resulting from eating lightly salted herring. But by far the highest numbers are in Japan, where up to 1,000 cases per year are reported. Fewer than 10 cases are reported in the United States each year.

How do I know I have it?
Symptoms occur anywhere up to two weeks after infection. In severe cases acute abdominal pain is felt as the worms burrow into the wall of the digestive tract. Nausea and vomiting are also common. Infected people often report feeling a tingling sensation in their throat just before they cough up a worm that has been crawling into the throat or nasal passages.

Chances of survival
The parasite is not life-threatening, but can be extremely painful, and is often misdiagnosed as appendicitis, Crohn's disease (see page 35) or as a gastric ulcer.

How do I get rid of it?
Severe infection requires surgery to remove the worms, although in most cases it is a matter of waiting for them to die.

What is it?

This disease primarily targets herbivorous mammals, but it can also be caught by birds and humans. It is caused by *Bacillus anthracis*, a spore-forming bacterium.

The disease is spread by the spores, which can lie dormant in the environment for years before entering the body in one of three ways: through a cut or abrasion on the skin (cutaneous), inhalation (lungs) or by swallowing (gastro-intestinal).

The cutaneous form of the disease is the most common, accounting for 95 percent of human cases worldwide.

Where can I catch it?

The disease occurs in sub-Sahelian Africa and Asia, parts of southern Europe, the Americas and Australia.

You can catch it directly or indirectly from infected animals, or by eating the undercooked meat of an infected animal, but there are no reported cases of human-to-human infection. It is also used as a weapon. Your symptoms will appear about one week after infection, but symptoms of inhalation anthrax may take up to six weeks to appear.

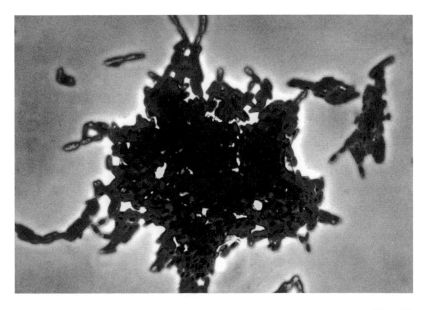

Major outbreaks
In October 2001, 22 people in the United States died from a terrorist attack that is thought to have originated in the mailroom of American Media Inc. in the town of Boca Raton, Florida.

The worst outbreak ever recorded occurred in Russia in 1979, when 79 cases of infection led to 68 reported deaths; it is thought to have been caused by the accidental release of *Bacillus anthracis* spores from a military base in Sverdlovsk.

How do I know I have it?
With cutaneous anthrax you develop a small sore that blisters and then becomes a swollen but painless ulcer with a black scab in the centre. Gastrointestinal anthrax causes nausea; you may vomit blood and have bloody diarrhea, fever and stomach ache. Inhalation anthrax causes flu-like symptoms and a headache, followed by chest pains and shortness of breath.

Chances of survival
If you have cutaneous anthrax, your chances of survival are good; even without treatment you have an 80 percent chance of recovery. But the other two forms are more serious, and your chances of survival are 25 percent if treated early, but usually fatal if left untreated.

How do I get rid of it?
A 60-day course of antibiotics such as ciprofloxacin, penicillin or doxycycline is very effective.

What is it?
Infection with a parasitic roundworm, *Ascaris lumbricoides*, which lives in the small intestine and can grow as thick as a pencil and up to 35 cm (13¾ in) in length.

Where can I catch it?
The eggs of the worm are excreted in the feces of infected people. In places where there are inadequate sewage systems or feces is used as fertiliser, the eggs can be swallowed when the feces contaminate soil, food or water and then finds its way into a person's mouth.

In the stomach, the worm larvae hatch from the eggs and travel to the lungs first via the intestinal wall, then through the blood or lymphatic system. They can be coughed up and swallowed or they climb up the bronchial tubes to the throat, and are then swallowed. After re-entering the intestines they develop into adult worms within about three months, mate and lay eggs.

Major outbreaks
It is the most prevalent human worm infection worldwide, especially in tropical and subtropical areas where sanitation is poor, and where entire populations may be infected.

How do I know I have it?
If you only have a few worms in your body, your symptoms may be mild or unnoticeable, including slight abdominal pain. The more worms you are harbouring the worse your symptoms. Some people may be infected with over 100 worms. If many worms infect your lungs at the same time, they will cause shortness of breath and even pneumonia. A lot of worms in the intestines will cause severe abdominal pain, vomiting and sometimes a complete intestinal blockage.

Chances of survival
Severe cases of infection can be fatal due to untreated pneumonia or intestinal blockage.

How do I get rid of it?
Without treatment, the worms will die after about two years, so long as you are not re-infected. It can be treated with drugs such as mebendazole or pyrantel pamoate.

What is it?
An infection, primarily of the lungs, an allergic reaction or a growth caused by the fungi *Aspergillus fumigatus* and *Aspergillus flavus*. Spores are inhaled and spread throughout the body in the blood stream, and can affect all major organs, as well as lodging in the eyes and ears.

Where can I catch it?
The fungus is found on dead leaves, grain stores, compost and other decaying vegetation. It can be detected in ventilation systems and building renovation projects. Virtually all of us have daily exposure to this fungus; the disease usually develops in patients with lowered immunity due to other conditions such as leukemia or AIDS. Transplant patients are particularly vulnerable.

Major outbreaks
As aspergillosis does not display distinct symptoms, it is believed to have been under-diagnosed. Labelled a rare disease until recently, the incidence is escalating. Modern methods of diagnosis, and immuno-supressing chemotherapy that leaves patients more vulnerable, are most likely to be the reason for the rise in cases.

How do I know I have it?
Allergic aspergillosis will make you feverish and wheezy, and you may cough up blood or mucous plugs. Invasive aspergillosis causes pneumonia: fever, chills, chest pain, a cough and shortness of breath. You may suffer with bone pain and detect blood in your urine and in your sputum. You will urinate less and will lose weight.

Chances of survival
Allergic aspergillosis generally is the more easily treatable form. Aspergillosis can cause blindness if it infects the eye. But invasive aspergillosis is by far the most serious, and the prognosis can be quite poor because patients have underlying medical conditions that are already compromising their immunity. Some studies indicate death rates of up to 95 percent in patients with AIDS or those who have undergone bone-marrow transplants.

How do I get rid of it?
Allergic aspergillosis is generally treated with anti-asthma drugs. Surgery may also be required for other forms of the disease and for the removal of fungal balls in the lungs that can develop in some post-tuberculosis patients.

Invasive aspergillosis can be treated with anti-fungal drugs, such as amphoterican, but two-thirds of people will not respond to this line of treatment. Alternative treatments include injecting anti-fungals directly into the lungs, or inhaling them through a nebulizer.

A further complication, hindering treatment in vulnerable patients, is that overuse of anti-fungal drugs has been found to lead to a drug-resistant aspergillosis, against which there is currently no effective treatment.

BABESIOSIS

What is it?
A rare infection of the red blood cells, resembling malaria, caused by the parasite *Babesia microti*.

Where can I catch it?
The disease is transmitted by the bite of an infected deer tick, or from transfusion from contaminated blood. Ticks generally cling to human skin, then climb to sheltered areas: the backs of knees, under the arms, between fingers and toes, for example.

Major outbreaks
Babesiosis is almost exclusively confined to the United States, although has been reported in parts of Europe (including the United Kingdom, Ireland and parts of eastern Europe) and Mexico. In the United States, it is most prevalent in the coastal areas of the Northeast, where a recent study of New Yorkers discovered *Babesia microti* antibodies in one percent of participants.

How do I know I have it?
In the majority of cases, babesiosis is a mild illness, and can even be symptom-free, but if you do suffer symptoms, you will begin to feel a general malaise: poor appetite and fatigue, progressing to headaches, fever, sweats and aching muscles. You may suffer from these symptoms for several days to several months, and you may even recover temporarily, only to fall ill again later.

Chances of survival
Babesiosis can be fatal, particularly where patients are elderly, have suppressed immunity or have had their spleen removed. It can cause a dramatic drop in blood pressure, severe anemia, liver problems and kidney failure.

How do I get rid of it?
Some patients will recover without treatment, but a course of anti-parasitic drugs is usually effective. There is no vaccine against the disease.

What is it?
A condition in women in which the healthy balance of bacteria is disrupted, causing one or more types to multiply excessively. One such bacterium is *Gardnerella vaginalis*.

Where can I catch it?
The mechanism is not fully understood but you can't get it from toilet seats, doorknobs and swimming pools, because the bacteria are already present in the vagina. Women who have never had sex rarely suffer from this condition, but the disease is not 'spread' by sex, although the risk of BV does increase in women who have multiple sex partners or use vaginal douches or intra-uterine contraceptive devices. It is more a case of BV occurring as a result of sexual contact rather than being passed on from one person to another.

Major outbreaks
BV is the most common vaginal infection in women of childbearing age. In the United States, as many as 16 percent of pregnant women have BV.

How do I know I have it?
Women may experience a strong fish-like odour (especially after intercourse), accompanied by vaginal discharge (white or grey), pain, itching or burning.

Chances of survival
BV rarely causes complications, but as with other sexually transmitted diseases (STDs), it increases a woman's suscepti-bility to HIV infection if she is exposed to the HIV virus. If the BV infects the uterus or fallopian tubes it causes pelvic inflammatory disease (see page 90) and increases the risk of complications during pregnancy (including low birth weight and premature birth).

How do I get rid of it?
Although BV may clear up without treatment, the antibiotics metronidazole or clindamycin should be used.

BELLS PALSY

What is it?
It is a weakness on one side of the face that often occurs because the stapedius muscle of the face becomes paralysed, but it can happen independently. It is named after Sir Charles Bell, the Scottish surgeon who discovered it.

Where can I catch it?
The most common cause is believed to be a complication of *herpes simplex* virus (the same virus that causes cold sores on your mouth), but other causes include diabetes, HIV infection, various cancers and the last trimester of pregnancy. But for three quarters of those affected, no cause can be found.

Major outbreaks
About one in 5,000 people develop it, but there haven't been any 'outbreaks' since it occurs with equal frequency worldwide, regardless of gender or race.

How do I know I have it?
One side of your face feels weak and droopy. You may not be able to close your eye, smile or wrinkle your forehead on that side. You may also experience a loss of taste at the front of your tongue or slurred speech and sounds may seem louder on the affected side. Another classic sign is tingling lips. Some sufferers only notice they have it when they look in the mirror.

Chances of survival
Bells palsy is not life-threatening, and three quarters of sufferers recover completely within three weeks. Ten percent still experience symptoms after six months, and many people develop synkinesis, which means that the corner of their mouth twitches when they blink.

How do I get rid of it?
Most people recover without treatment, but it is essential to keep the affected eye wet with eye drops to compensate for the inability to blink. Sometimes the eyelids are sewn together for protection while the sufferer recovers. A strong steroid such as Prednisone may be administered and a course of antiviral treatment and vitamin supplements.

What is it?

A contagious disease of animals caused by type A viruses that normally infect only birds (especially domestic poultry) and sometimes pigs.

The disease in birds takes two forms. The first causes mild illness, but the second form, known as 'highly pathogenic avian influenza' (first recognised in Italy in 1878), is extremely contagious in birds and fatal.

Type A viruses don't usually infect humans, but there have been several human infections since 1997. As yet there are no instances of bird flu having jumped from human to human.

Where can I catch it?

Cambodia, China, Hong Kong, Indonesia, Japan, Korea, Laos, Thailand, Vietnam.

Major outbreaks

In 1997 in Hong Kong, strain H5N1 infected both chickens and, for the first time, humans. Out of the 18 people who were hospitalised, six died. Authorities responded by culling over 1.5 million chickens.

Since 2003, outbreaks in poultry caused by the H5N1 strain have occurred in Korea, Vietnam, Japan, Thailand, Cambodia, China, Laos and Indonesia.

How do I know I have it?

The reported symptoms of avian influenza in humans have ranged from typical influenza-like symptoms (e.g., fever, cough, sore throat and muscle aches) to eye infections, pneumonia, acute respiratory distress, viral pneumonia and other severe and life-threatening complications.

Chances of survival

If you're a bird, your chances of survival are virtually nil; for humans it is about 30 percent.

How do I get rid of it?

The WHO has reported that several pharmaceutical companies are attempting to isolate the virus and make a vaccine for humans, but this is still several months away.

BLASTOMYCOSIS
(North American Blastomycosis, Gilchrist's Disease,
Chicago Disease or Namekagon River Fever)

What is it?
An infection caused by the fungus *Blastomyces dermatitidis*, which is found in moist acidic soil. As well as humans, it can infect cats, dogs and other animals.

Where can I catch it?
You can either breathe in the airborne spores of the fungus or they can enter the body through a cut or scratch. You can't 'catch' it from another person or animal. Most people are resistant and their natural defences can fight off the fungus before it can cause illness.

It is endemic in parts of the Southcentral, Southeastern and Midwestern United States along the Mississippi and Ohio Rivers. It is also found in Central and South America and Africa.

Major outbreaks
Distribution is worldwide, but it is very rare. There have only been 12 documented cases in the United States.

How do I know I have it?
Symptoms may take up to three months to appear. The disease usually infects the lungs, but it can also affect the eyes, skin, reproductive tract and bones. Most people develop flu-like symptoms with fever, cough, yellow or green spit, aching muscles and chest pain and some develop crusted, ulcerated pimples and/or pneumonia.

Chances of survival
Complications include permanent lung damage, pulmonary infection and widespread infection of critical organs. The mortality rate is about 5 percent if treated, rising to 40 percent if untreated.

How do I get rid of it?
If you are misdiagnosed with tuberculosis (TB, see page 132) you may be given antibacterial antibiotics, which will make you worse. Anti-fungal medication such as Itraconazole should be used for several weeks to months.

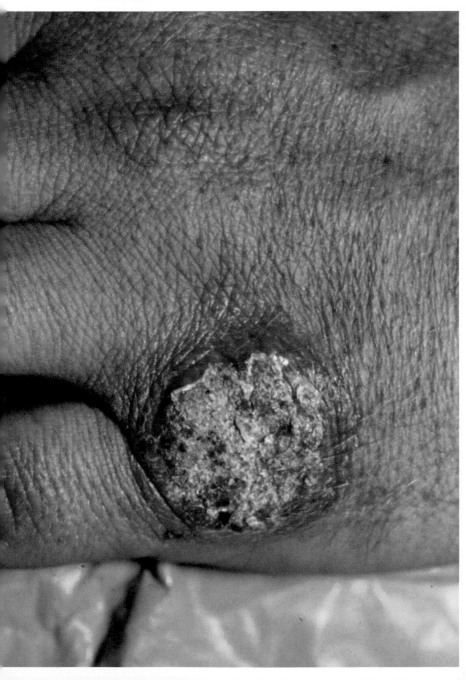

BOVINE SPONGIFORM ENCEPHALOPATHY AND NEW VARIANT CREUTZFELDT-JAKOB DISEASE

What is it?
Bovine Spongiform Encephalopathy (BSE or 'Mad Cow disease') is a progressive neurological disease in cattle that has been linked as a cause of New Variant Creutzfeldt-Jakob disease (vCJD) in humans. vCJD is a rare degenerative brain disorder. (It is distinct from the standard form of CJD that affects an older population and is endemic throughout the world.)

Where can I catch it?
Eating the meat of cattle infected with BSE is thought to be the predominant means of contracting vCJD. There is also evidence that blood transfusions from a donor infected with vCJD can also cause infection. The disease has a very long incubation period, with infected people remaining asymptomatic for years. All cases of vCJD to date have occurred where people have lived in a country where BSE has been diagnosed in cattle. In the United Kingdom the average age of patients with vCJD was 28 years.

Major outbreaks
vCJD is a very rare disease, with 147 cases reported across the United Kingdom, Ireland, Canada, Italy and the United States between 1995 and 2004.

With the exception of cases in Italy, all other cases outside the United Kingdom were because patients had been exposed to BSE infected meat in the United Kingdom.

How do I know I have it?
You will feel depressed, have coordination problems and may have short-term memory loss and mood swings. You will have pins and needles in your arms and legs, severe headaches, cold hands and feet and painful feet. The nature of many of the early symptoms means that many patients are referred first to a psychiatrist, rather than a neurologist.

Chances of survival
New Variant Creutzfeldt-Jakob disease is fatal.

How do I get rid of it?
There is currently no treatment for vCJD.

What is it?

An infectious disease caused by the bacteria of the genus *Brucella*. It has been described for centuries, and it is named after British Army physician David Bruce, who isolated the bacteria in 1887.

Where can I catch it?

Various types of *Brucella* bacteria affect animals including sheep, goats, cattle, deer, pigs and dogs. Humans become infected when they come into contact with an infected animal, either by breathing in the airborne bacteria, eating or drinking infected food products (e.g., unpasteurized milk or cheese) or when bacteria enter the skin through a cut or scratch. It is rare to catch brucellosis from another person.

Major outbreaks

It is found worldwide, and high-risk areas include the Mediterranean Basin, South and Central America, Eastern Europe, Asia, Africa, the Caribbean and the Middle East. Brucellosis is rare in the United States, where about 100 cases are reported each year.

How do I know I have it?

Between one to eight weeks after infection you will experience flu-like symptoms including fever, headaches, back pain and weakness, depression and irritability. In rare cases, the central nervous system and heart may be affected and recurrent fevers and joint pain may persist for months. A blood or bone-marrow test will confirm the diagnosis.

Chances of survival

Only about two percent of sufferers die from endocarditis (infection of the interior lining of the heart). It has been developed as a biological weapon because only a few bacteria are required to cause infection.

How do I get rid of it?

Antibiotics such as doxycycline and rifampicin are used for six weeks to prevent recurring infection.

What is it?

It is ulceration caused by an organism called *Mycobacterium ulcerans*, which is part of the same family of bacteria that cause TB and leprosy. It usually attacks the skin and underlying tissues of the limbs and can cause major deformities.

It was first detected in 1948 in Australia, where it was called 'Bairnsdale ulcer', but as early as 1897 cases were reported in Uganda.

Where can I catch it?

'Buruli' is the name of an area of Uganda where the disease is very common, and there were many cases in the 1960s, but it is now endemic to most parts of West Africa and is also found in Asia, Latin America and the Western Pacific.

Major outbreaks

In the 1960s and 1970s, many cases were reported in Uganda, the Democratic Republic of the Congo and Papua New Guinea.

How do I know I have it?

The first signs are painless hard nodules beneath the surface of your skin. The bacteria produce a toxin that destroys tissue and affects your immune system. Within a few weeks large areas of your skin, tissue, nerves and even bone may be eaten away.

Chances of survival

It isn't usually life-threatening and the lesions will eventually heal themselves, but without early treatment you will be left with serious deformities and scarring that may affect you ability to move your limbs; plus you will be at risk for secondary infections.

How do I get rid of it?

Antibiotics have little effect on Buruli ulcers. Research has shown that a combination of an aminoglycoside (amikacin or streptomycin) and rifampicin cures Buruli ulcer in mice, but currently, surgery to remove the ulcer (before it grows bigger) followed by skin grafts is the only effective treatment.

What is it?
A parasitic disease caused by the parasite, *Trypanosoma cruzi*, which is related to the protozoa that cause African trypanosomiasis (see page 7). It is named after Carlos Chagas, the Brazilian doctor who described the disease in 1909.

Where can I catch it?
It is found only in Mexico and South America. The parasite can enter your body in three ways. The Assassin bugs that live in the walls of houses in poor areas can emerge at night and suck your blood. Its feces contain the parasite, which can enter the bite wound when you scratch it. You can also catch it through a transfusion of infected blood, or a mother can pass it to her fetus in utero.

Major outbreaks
Over 20 million people are infected, and about 25 percent of the population of Latin America are at risk of catching the disease.

How do I know I have it?
You will probably develop a small sore where the parasite entered your body.

If this is near your eye, your eyelid will swell (this is called Romaña's sign). This is followed a few days later by the acute phase, including fever and swollen lymph nodes, which may be fatal, especially to young children. If you survive, you will enter the chronic symptomless stage, which may last several years, during which the parasite enters most of your organs and causes severe damage to your heart, intestines and lungs.

Chances of survival
If the acute phase doesn't kill you, you will have a 30 percent chance of developing chronic symptoms, sometimes many years later, including heart disease (leading to heart failure) and digestive problems, difficulty swallowing and subsequent malnutrition.

How do I get rid of it?
You must be treated during the acute phase, with either benznidazole or the more experimental nifurtimox.

CHLAMYDIA

What is it?

A bacterial infection of the reproductive organs caused by *Chlamydia trachomatis*, which can affect men and women. Symptoms are usually mild or absent, although serious complications can occur, leaving permanent damage.

Where can I catch it?

Chlamydia is transmitted by sexual intercourse with an infected person, or by close personal contact. It can also be passed through the birth canal to an unborn child.

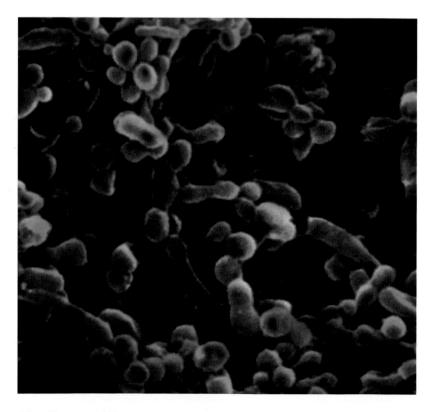

Major outbreaks

In the United States, chlamydia is the most frequently reported STD, affecting five percent of the adult population and 10 percent of sexually active adolescent females by 2003. Every year 2.8 million Americans become infected with chlamydia.

How do I know I have it?

Known as the 'silent disease', an estimated 80 percent of women and 50 percent of men won't know they are infected at all. If you do develop symptoms, you are likely to do so within three weeks of exposure. In women, you will suffer with bleeding after intercourse or between menstrual periods, lower abdominal pain, vaginal discharge and painful urination. Men will notice a discharge from the penis and a burning or itching around the opening of the penis. You may develop an inflamed testicle, due to an infected duct and you will suffer from painful burning during urination. Men and women may notice an increased need to urinate. Chlamydia will cause infection in the rectum following anal sex and in the throat after oral sex.

Chances of survival

This is not a life-threatening bacterial infection, although women with chlamydia are five times more likely to become infected with HIV if exposed. If the disease is left untreated, up to 40 percent of women will develop pelvic inflammatory disease (PID), which can cause permanent damage to the fallopian tubes, uterus and surrounding tissues. PID sufferers experience chronic pelvic pain and are at greater risk of infertility and potentially fatal ectopic pregnancy (see also page 90). Rarely, genital chlamydial infections in men can cause sterility and sexually acquired reactive arthritis (Reiter syndrome).

Babies born to infected mothers are more prone to respiratory tract and eye infections. It is a major cause of pneumonia in early infancy.

How do I get rid of it?

A single-dose antibiotic, such as azithromycin, or a weeklong course of, for example, doxycycline will cure chlamydia in approximately 95 percent of cases.

CHOLERA

What is it?
A bacterial infection of the small intestine caused by *Vibrio cholerae*, which leads to extremely watery diarrhea.

Where can I catch it?
The most common cause is drinking contaminated water or eating conta-minated food (especially shellfish). Cholera is common in areas where large populations are crowded together in unsanitary conditions without access to clean drinking water; it usually accompanies war and famine, or natural disasters such as floods or earthquakes; it is endemic in India, Asia, Africa, the Mediterranean and South America.

Major outbreaks
Cholera has been around for centuries, and is even mentioned in Greek and Sanskrit writing. In 1848, 5,000 deaths were caused by an outbreak in New York, but no major outbreaks have occurred in the United States since 1911. Elsewhere in the world, cholera outbreaks accompany famine, war and natural disasters. For example, in April 1997, 90,000 Rwandan refugees were affected.

How do I know I have it?
A mild bout of cholera will cause few symptoms, but a severe infection will cause leg and stomach cramps, vomiting and a massive quantity of fishy-smelling watery diarrhea. You'll lose about a litre of liquid every hour. The only solids you'll pass will resemble bits of rice (these are actually flakes of mucus, epithelial cells and bacteria). You may also have a very rapid heartbeat.

Chances of survival
Acute cholera is fatal if left untreated because of severe and rapid dehydration, so it is essential to replace the fluids and electrolytes (the body's salts and minerals), usually through an intravenous drip.

How do I get rid of it?
Tetracycline and other antibiotics may be used to shorten the symptoms, but you've got to let it run its course; you will make a full recovery as long as you are kept hydrated.

CHRONIC FATIGUE SYNDROME (CFS)

What is it?

A complex disorder with a spectrum of debilitating symptoms, resulting in chronic fatigue that does not improve with bed rest and that is often made worse by physical or mental exertion.

Where can I catch it?

For many people CFS begins after a period of illness such as a cold or a stomach bug. Others link its onset to a period of high stress, while some find it creeps up on them slowly over several months.

It used to be called 'yuppie flu' because in the early 1980s, many well-educated, well-off women in their 30s were going down with it. Now it is recognised that it affects men and women of all ages and social classes and races, although twice as many women than men.

Major outbreaks

Similar illnesses have been reported as far back as the 19th century. The Center for Disease Control (CDC) estimates that as many as 500,000 people in the United States have CFS and several million worldwide have it.

How do I know I have it?

Because it is so difficult to pin down, a 1994 group of CFS researchers drafted a list of symptoms. First you must have been experiencing chronic fatigue for at least six months and have ruled out other medical conditions.

Second, you must have at least two of these symptoms: marked reduction in short-term memory or concentration; sore throat; tender lymph nodes; muscle pain; multi-joint pain without swelling or redness; headaches of a new type, pattern or severity; unrefreshing sleep and post-exertional malaise lasting more than 24 hours. The symptoms must have

persisted or recurred during six or more consecutive months of illness and must not have predated the fatigue.

Chances of survival

It is not fatal, but its effects can last for years.

How do I get rid of it?

Five years after diagnosis, about 50 percent of sufferers consider themselves to have 'recovered', but for the other half it's a matter of managing their illness; they may have times when they can function normally, followed by periods when their symptoms return. Others get progressively worse.

A major part of coming to terms with the illness is education, and modifying one's behaviour so as not to aggravate the symptoms.

CONDYLOMATA ACUMINATA

What is it?
An infection of the genitals caused by the Human Papillomavirus (HPV), also known as genital or venereal warts.

Where can I catch it?
Genital warts are highly contagious and are transmitted by skin-to-skin contact during oral, vaginal or anal sex with an infected partner.

Major outbreaks
Some health experts believe that the HPV is responsible for more sexually transmitted infections per year than any other STD. It is thought that about 20 million Americans are currently affected.

How do I know I have it?
Many HPV infections are asymptomatic, and there are about 30 forms of the virus that can be spread through sexual contact. Genital warts are the easiest form of HPV infection to recognise. You will see one or more soft, moist, flesh-coloured bumps in the vulva, cervix or vagina in women, or on the penis, scrotum or anus in men. Multiple warts may merge and appear cauliflower-like. If you cannot see signs of warts, but know you have been exposed to the virus, covering the area with vinegar will make any 'invisible' warts appear white.

Chances of survival
Genital warts themselves will often clear up without treatment, but they can be an indication of a more widespread HPV infection, which can include cancer of the cervix, anus or penis. Genital warts can cause complications during pregnancy, as they can grow to obstruct the vagina, making delivery more difficult. Babies born to women with genital warts can develop a potentially life-threatening form of infection in their throats called laryngeal papillomatosis and will need frequent laser surgery to stop the warts from blocking their airways.

How do I get rid of it?
Genital warts can be removed by freezing them or burning them off with chemicals or electrolysis. Minor surgery or laser treatment may also be used. If removal does not prevent them from recurring, you may be given the drug interferon that will stop the symptoms, although you will still carry the virus in your body.

What is it?

A chronic inflammation affecting the digestive system, typically the lower part of the small intestine or the colon.

Where can I catch it?

There are no proven theories about the causes of Crohn's disease, although in about 20 percent of cases, it develops in relatives of patients with irritable bowel syndrome (IBS) in some form. First symptoms typically develop in your 20s.

Major outbreaks

The disease occurs worldwide, regardless of gender or race.

How do I know I have it?

You are most likely to experience pain in the lower right-hand side of your stomach and diarrhea, and you may also notice rectal bleeding, fever, loss of appetite and weight loss. Bleeding can be persistent enough to lead to anemia. Crohn's disease can cause development delay and stunted growth in children.

Ulceration in affected parts of the intestine can spread to affect the bladder, vagina, anus or rectum, developing into fistulas, which may need treatment with medication or surgery as they easily become infected.

Chances of survival

Crohn's patients experience periods of remission, sometimes lasting years, during which time they remain symptom free. Predicting recurrence or remission is impossible. However the majority of patients lead normal lives, have families and hold down jobs successfully.

Occasionally surgery may be recommended to remove part of the intestine, and in cases where the Crohn's disease affects the large intestine, a colectomy is sometimes performed, removing the entire colon and replacing it with a waste pouch worn over a small opening (a stoma) in the lower abdomen.

How do I get rid of it?

Crohn's disease cannot be cured, although medication (aminosalicylates and corticosteroids) can control symptoms. Surgery is not preventative, as the disease will often recur in the area of the intestine next to the section removed.

DENGUE

What is it?
Dengue fever is a mild viral illness
transmitted by mosquitoes (especially
Aedes aegypti). It causes a fever, rash
and aching muscles and joints. However,
it is caused by several related viruses,
and if you have become infected by one
of them after already acquiring immunity
to another, you may develop dengue
hemorrhagic fever, which can be fatal.

Where can I catch it?
It occurs in tropical and subtropical
regions, including Southeast Asia, the
Indonesian archipelago into northeastern
Australia, parts of sub-Saharan Africa
and parts of South and Central America.

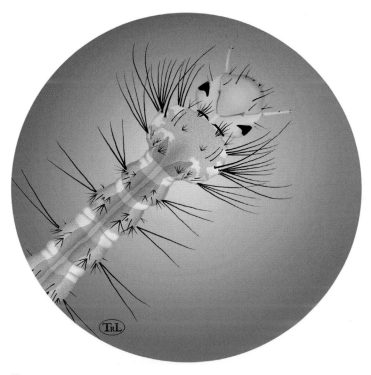

Major outbreaks

More than 100 million cases of dengue fever occur worldwide each year and a small number of these cases develop into dengue hemorrhagic fever.

How do I know I have it?

First you will develop a high fever, up to 40°C (104°F), and a headache. You may get a red rash over most of your body during the fever, and later you'll have joint and muscle pains. You may also develop a second measles-like rash. Your skin will feel ultra sensitive, and you will feel very uncomfortable.

If you are one of the unlucky minority to contract the more serious dengue hemorrhagic fever, you will show the same early signs, but you will also become very irritable, restless and sweaty after a few days, then your body will go into shock as pinpoint spots of blood appear on the surface of your skin and larger patches form underneath.

Chances of survival

You should make a full recover from dengue fever, but the hemorrhagic fever may kill you during the shock period.

How do I get rid of it?

You just have to let it run its course. Prevention is the best cure, by avoiding mosquito bites and using protective clothing and insect repellents. There is no vaccine at present.

DIPHTHERIA

What is it?

This disease is caused by *Corynebacterium diphtheriae* bacteria. Respiratory diphtheria attacks the throat and nose and cutaneous diphtheria attacks the skin. They are both highly contagious.

Where can I catch it?

It is common in many parts of the world where widespread vaccination does not occur, including the Caribbean and Latin America. It is spread by breathing in the bacteria after an infected person sneezes or coughs, or through contact with their saliva or nasal secretions.

Major outbreaks

Recent outbreaks have occurred in China, Algeria and Ecuador. It has reached epidemic proportions in the former Soviet republics.

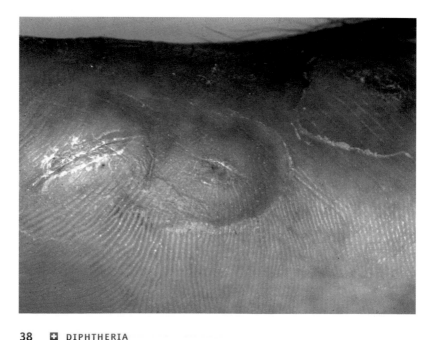

How do I know I have it?

Between two and four days after infection, you will develop a sore throat and mild fever, but it is usually accompanied by swollen lymph glands, so your neck will swell considerably. Also, a membrane forms over your tonsils and throat that makes breathing and swallowing difficult. Some people present no symptoms, but remain very contagious.

Chances of survival

Complications include inflammation of your heart and several nerves, leading to lung paralysis, pain and muscle wasting. One in 10 people suffering from respiratory diphtheria die; cutaneous diphtheria is less serious and is rarely fatal.

How do I get rid of it?

Without treatment the bacteria produces a dangerous toxin, which causes the complications mentioned above. You should be injected with an antitoxin (made from horse serum) to neutralize the poison and antibiotics to fight the bacteria. If you have acute symptoms, you may need to be put on a respirator.

What is it?
Infection by a parasitic worm, *Dracunculus medinensis*. This ancient disease is mentioned in a 3,500-year-old Egyptian medical text, and a Sanskrit poem of a similar age declares 'Let not the sinuous worm strike me nor wound my foot'.

The miniscule larvae of the guinea worm infect a tiny water flea called cyclops. If you drink unfiltered or untreated water that has been infected with this flea, you will ingest the larvae. The male larvae grow and mate in your abdominal tissue while the females usually move to the lower limbs and feet, where they grow up to three feet long before bursting out of the skin.

Where can I catch it?
It used to be prevalent worldwide, but now it is mainly confined to poor rural areas of sub-Saharan Africa, where there are inadequate supplies of clean drinking water, especially southern Sudan, although there have been a few cases in India and Yemen.

Major outbreaks
Thanks to the efforts of UNICEF, the WHO and other organisations, infection has fallen significantly from the estimated 3.5 million cases in the 1980s to about 150,000 today.

How do I know I have it?
For the first year after infection you will have no idea what is growing inside you. The only warning signs are a fever and swelling at the places where the worms are about to emerge. You'll then develop a painful blister; as soon as it is immersed in water the worms will break through the skin, and you'll spend the next several months trying to remove them. This is usually done by carefully winding each worm around a stick, being careful not to snap them; otherwise they will retreat into your body and cause severe inflammation. Sometimes a worm can be removed in a matter of days, but it usually takes much longer, and you'll be incapacitated for weeks, even months.

Chances of survival
Your chances of survival are good, but you may be left with permanent crippling after a long period of agony. Complications can be caused by an infected wound, and some people die from tetanus (see page 124).

How do I get rid of it?
There is no vaccine or cure once you have been infected other than waiting in agony for the worms to leave your body. Sometimes they can be surgically removed and you would benefit from antihistamines to reduce the swelling and antibiotics to prevent infection.

DYSENTERY

What is it?
A mild to severe bowel infection that causes diarrhea that contains blood and mucus.

Where can I catch it?
The two main types of dysentery are shigellosis (caused by one of four Shigella bacteria) and the less common amoebic dysentery (caused by the amoeba *Entamoeba histolytica*). The former is highly contagious and can be spread by inanimate objects such as toilet seats, clothes and doorknobs (don't let anyone tell you that you can't catch stuff from toilet seats). The latter is transmitted by contaminated water.

Major outbreaks
As with cholera and malaria, an outbreak of dysentery usually accompanies poverty and poor sanitation in underdeveloped nations or anywhere where large groups of people are displaced and crowded together following war or natural disasters. In developed countries the strains of Shigella bacteria are milder, so many cases aren't reported.

How do I know I have it?
One to three days after infection, you'll have copious amount of bloody diarrhea, which will later reduce in volume, but not frequency. You will usually experience severe stomach cramps and nausea, fever and rectal pain. In rare cases you may suffer blood poisoning, seizures, kidney failure, liver infection and intestinal ulceration and abscesses.

Chances of survival
Between five and 15 percent of cases of shigellosis are fatal. It is important to avoid severe dehydration caused by loss of fluids.

How do I get rid of it?
You will usually recover with adequate fluids and without antibiotic treatment, but it is a good idea to take some, since your stools will be highly contagious for several weeks (norfloxacin, ampicillin and cotrimaxozole for shigellosis and metronidazole for amoebic dysentery). Anti-diarrhea products such as Imodium or Lomotil should be avoided.

What is it?
A rare viral disease affecting the central nervous system.

Where can I catch it?
The disease is spread to humans and horses via a mosquito common to the east coast of the United States and the eastern Gulf coastline. Cases have also been reported in Central and South America and the Caribbean.

Major outbreaks
EEE is rare, with an average annual diagnosis of around five cases in the United States.

How do I know I have it?
In most cases, EEE is without symptoms. You may only suffer mildly, with a fever, severe muscle shakes for a few days, a headache and a sore throat that lasts up to two weeks. If the infection spreads to the central nervous system, however, you will quickly deteriorate, with a severe headache, vomiting and diarrhea, restlessness and loss of appetite, leading to seizures and constant tremors, twitching and a rigid neck before falling into a coma.

Chances of survival
For patients whose nervous system becomes infected, the prognosis is bleak. Fifty percent of these patients will die, and permanent brain damage reduces the majority of others to a lifetime of physical and mental dependency. These cases seem to occur in patients under the age of 15 years and above the age of 50.

How do I get rid of it?
The milder infections require no treatment. However there is currently no known treatment available for those with severe symptoms. There are no anti-viral drugs that will attack EEE, and antibiotics will have no effect.

EBOLA
HEMORRHAGIC FEVER

What is it?

One of the most virulent viral diseases known to humankind with up to a 90 percent fatality rate. It is classified as a Level-4 pathogen, which is higher than AIDS. It is caused by one of several Ebola viruses, and it was named in 1976 after the river in Democratic Republic of the Congo (formally Zaire) where it was first detected.

Where can I catch it?

Limited to parts of Africa: Sudan, Zaire, Ivory Coast, Democratic Republic of the Congo and Gabon. It is transmitted by contact with the blood, body fluids and tissues of infected people or animals (such as chimpanzees, gorillas, forest antelope and porcupines). Scientists think that bats may play a major part in incubating the virus, because they do not die when infected. Latest research suggests that one strain of the virus, *E. Zaire*, may be airborne transmissible.

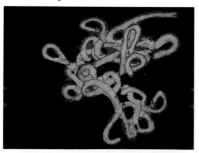

Major outbreaks

Since it was discovered, 1,850 cases have been recorded with over 1,200 deaths.

How do I know I have it?

Your symptoms will appear between two and 21 days after infection. These include a sudden fever, extreme weakness, muscle pain, headache and sore throat, followed by vomiting and diarrhea. Then a hemorrhagic rash (containing blood) develops over your entire body, and often your gastrointestinal tract will start bleeding, so blood will come out of your mouth, and blood and intestinal lining will come out from your anus.

Chances of survival

Not good. Mortality is high, reaching 90 percent. You will usually die from shock rather than loss of blood.

How do I get rid of it?

There is no known vaccine, cure or treatment. If you're unlucky enough to be infected, the main priority is to prevent its spread, because the chances are you will soon die.

What is it?

An acute disease caused by Ehrlichia bacteria, especially *ehrlichia chaffeensis*, which infects the white blood cells. Ehrlichia is part of the Rickettsiae family of bacteria, which are associated with Rocky Mountain spotted fever (see page 107) and typhus.

Where can I catch it?

It is transmitted to humans through the bite of an infected tick. People who spend a lot of time outdoors in tick-infested areas are at greatest risk. Ehrlichia is associated with specific ticks such as the Lone Star tick, the American dog tick and two deer ticks. A tick must be attached for several hours to transmit the disease, so vigilance and early removal is recommended.

Major outbreaks

In the United States, Ehrlichiosis is found mainly in the southern central states and the Southeast.

How do I know I have it?

Symptoms typically occur between one and three weeks after infection and range from fever, muscle pain, severe headache and chills to nausea, vomiting, mental confusion and a skin rash. A blood test will confirm infection and show a low white blood cell count and antibodies.

Chances of survival

The disease can be fatal, especially in elderly victims, but full recovery is expected with treatment, although it may damage various organs, especially the lungs and kidneys.

How do I get rid of it?

Rickettsial diseases are treated with tetracycline antibiotics.

ELEPHANTIASIS
(Lymphatic Filariasis)

What is it?

It is a lymphatic system disorder caused by parasitic worms. The most common culprits are *Wuchereria bancrofti, Brugia malayi* and *B. timori*. The worm larvae are transmitted into a person's bloodstream when they are bitten by a carrier mosquito. The larvae then reproduce and spread through the bloodstream for many years until symptoms finally appear.

As millions of the parasites accumulate in the blood vessels and lymph glands, they can restrict circulation and cause fluid retention, leading to excessively swollen arms, legs, genitals and breasts.

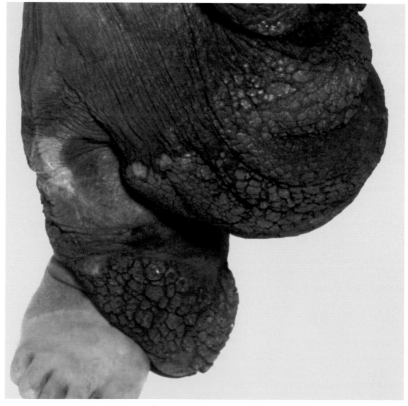

Where can I catch it?
It is most prevalent in tropical regions
and particularly in parts of Africa.

Major outbreaks
Approximately 170 million people in
the tropical and subtropical areas of
Southeast Asia, South America, Africa
and Pacific islands are affected. It is the
second leading cause of permanent and
longterm disability in the world.

How do I know I have it?
The scrotum swells up or the vuvla
becomes massive and tumorous. You
may also suffer gross enlargement of
limbs, trunk or head, your skin will
become thick, dark, pebbly and
ulcerated and you will feel feverish.

Chances of survival
Very good. The disease is rarely fatal,
just horribly disfiguring.

How do I get rid of it?
You can get treatment to slow down
the symptoms, but at the moment there
is no cure. You could try a few doses of

chemotherapy to attack the adult
worms and benzopyrone drugs, which
may reduce swelling, but you can
probably only get them on the black
market because several deaths have
been attributed to their use.

FASCIOLIASIS

What is it?
Infection with liver flukes, the trematodes *Fasciola hepatica* and *Fasciola gigantica*, which infect various animals, mostly herbivores.

Where can I catch it?
The adult flukes live in the bile ducts of mammals, and eggs are discharged in their stools. The eggs develop inside freshwater snails, and then encyst on freshwater plants. A person becomes infected by accidentally swallowing the liver fluke cysts that are found in the soil or on poorly washed freshwater plants such as watercress, mint, parsley and water lettuce. There have also been reported cases of infection by eating uncooked or raw liver from infected sheep, goats and cows.

Major outbreaks
There are an estimated two million cases worldwide, and incidents are highest in areas where sheep and cattle are raised. Hot spots include Bolivia, Ecuador, Peru and Egypt.

How do I know I have it?
Once the cysts have been swallowed the larvae travel through the intestinal wall into the bile ducts. During this process an infected person suffers abdominal pain, fever, vomiting and diarrhea. It takes about four months for the flukes to mature into adults.

Chances of survival
It is seldom fatal, but without treatment a person may become severely anemic, experience weight loss and suffer chronic damage to their liver and gallbladder.

How do I get rid of it?
Drug treatment with triclabendazole or bithionol.

What is it?

Giant intestinal flukes, several centimetres in length, which attach themselves to the intestinal wall.

Where can I catch it?

The fluke is common to pigs in the Far East, especially Thailand, Vietnam, China, Taiwan, Indonesia, India and Bangladesh. The flukes in pig intestines release eggs in their stools that, on reaching fresh water, take up residence in freshwater snails, where they develop into larvae. The larvae then pass from the snails to form larval cysts in fresh-water plants such as water chestnuts. Human consumption of the raw plant will release flukes into the intestine.

Major outbreaks

Infection is most common in school-aged children in areas where pig rearing and the consumption of freshwater plants coincide. Studies estimate a 57 percent infection of children in China, 60 percent in India and 50 percent in Bangladesh.

How do I know I have it?

In most cases, you will not know you have it, as infections are often asymptomatic. In more severe infections however, you will have abdominal pain, diarrhea or constipation, nausea and loss of appetite. Your face and body may swell and you may also be anemic. These symptoms will develop several months after ingesting the cysts.

Chances of survival

Infection is not life-threatening, although severe infections can cause malnutrition in children.

How do I get rid of it?

Fasciolopsiasis is treatable with a single dose of the anti-worm drug, praziquantel.

What is it?

A mild rash-causing illness caused by the parvovirus B19, which most commonly affects children. It is called Fifth disease because in the 1800s, an attempt was made to classify various childhood rashes in terms of their contagiousness. It was rash illness number five (measles, Scarlet fever, Rubella and Duke's disease are the first four).

Where can I catch it?

It is spread by close contact with the saliva or nasal secretions when an infected person sneezes or coughs, or by sharing cups or utensils. Once the rash appears the person is no longer infectious. It affects only humans and cannot be caught or transmitted by animals.

Major outbreaks

It is found worldwide, although 50 percent of the population is immune due to prior infection.

How do I know I have it?

Within two weeks after infection a child will show mild flu-like symptoms, followed a few days later by a 'slapped-cheek' rash on the face, while a lacy red rash may appear on the rest of the body. The rash disappears within about 10 days. Adults tend to develop painfully joints rather than a rash. Twenty percent of those infected show no symptoms at all.

Chances of survival

It is not life-threatening, except to people with a suppressed immune system or chronic anemia (such as sickle-cell anemia). Women who develop fifth disease during pregnancy have a five to 10 percent risk of their unborn child developing anemia, as the disease attacks the baby's bone marrow, but it does not cause birth defects.

How do I get rid of it?

The disease will resolve itself without treatment. Only those with complications require hospitalisation (and blood transfusions in the case of anemia). There is no vaccination.

What is it?
A STD caused by the herpes simplex viruses type 1 (HSV-1), and more commonly type 2 (HSV-2). It is one of the fastest growing infectious diseases in the world.

Where can I catch it?
It is transmitted from an infected person during sex, regardless of whether or not they have herpes sores. So it is possible for people to spread the disease without knowing they have it. It is very rarely, if at all, spread by touching shared objects such as a doorknob or toilet seat.

Major outbreaks
The disease is present worldwide. In the United States, at least 45 million people have had genital HSV infection. It is more common in women than men, due to the fact that it is easier for women to catch it from men than vice-versa.

How do I know I have it?
HSV-1 can cause genital sores, but usually presents as infections of the mouth and lips (cold sores). Most genital herpes is caused by HSV-2 and shows up as several blisters on and around the genitals that burst to become ulcers that clear up after about month.

The infection can stay in your nerve cells for the rest of your life, so you may experience several outbreaks of sores (typically about four or five during the first year), each time getting progressively less severe and less frequent over time.

Many people show no symptoms, while others experience an itching or burning feeling in the genitals, fluid discharge, swollen glands, mild fever and headaches.

Chances of survival
Herpes can only be fatal in rare cases where a fetus is infected because its mother contracts herpes during pregnancy. Herpes infection also increases a person's susceptibility to HIV, if exposed to the virus.

How do I get rid of it?
There is no cure for genital herpes. Once infected you have it for life, although it may be latent and cause no further symptoms.

What is it?
A diarrheal infection of the intestine caused by *Giardia intenstinalis*, a single-celled microscopic parasite. It is one of the most common waterborne diseases and the most frequent cause of non-bacterial diarrhea in the United States.

Where can I catch it?
The most common cause is through swallowing infected water (swimming or drinking) or swallowing something that has come into contact with the feces of an infected person. The parasite has a protective outer shell that enables it to live outside the body for a long time, and it can also be picked up from surfaces. The parasite lives in the intestine and releases cysts into the stool.

Major outbreaks
Giardiasis is found worldwide and every-where within the United States, and it is more prevalent in children than adults, although adults show more chronic symptoms.

How do I know I have it?
Some people experience no symptoms, but an infection often causes diarrhea, flatulence, stomach cramps, nausea and floating greasy stools. Symptoms appear about a week after infection and may last up to six weeks.

Chances of survival
It is important to drink plenty of fluids to prevent dehydration; otherwise it is not life-threatening. It is very contagious, so it is vital that infected people wash their hands well after visiting the bathroom or before eating or handling food, and they should avoid swimming.

How do I get rid of it?
The infection will disappear without treatment so long as scrupulous hygiene is maintained to avoid re-infection.

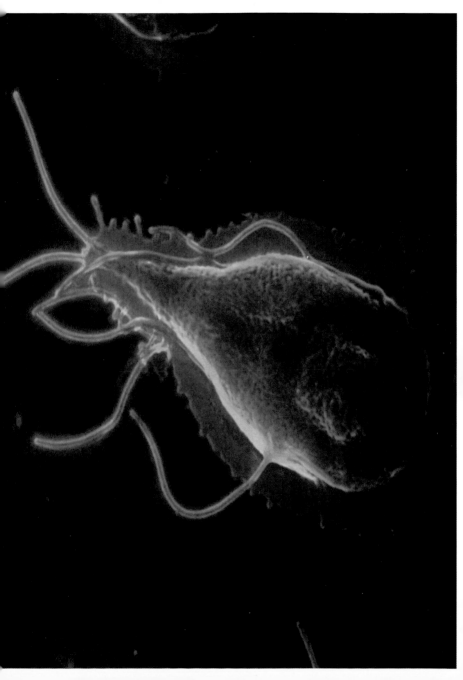

What is it?
A STD caused by *Neisseria gonorrhea*, a bacterium that grows in mucous areas of the body. These include the reproductive tract, uterus and fallopian tubes in women and in the urethra, throat, eyes and anus of both sexes.

Where can I catch it?
Anyone who is sexually active can contract the disease. It is spread through contact with the penis, vagina, mouth or anus of an infected person, regardless of whether ejaculation takes place. A previous infection does not give someone immunity from catching it again.

Major outbreaks
About 70 million cases occur each year worldwide. More than 700,000 new cases of gonorrhea occur in the United States each year, most commonly among the 15-to-35 age group.

How do I know I have it?
Symptoms, if any, appear between two to 30 days after infection. In men, these include a burning sensation when urinating and a yellowish-white discharge from the penis, and some men get painfully swollen testicles. Symptoms in women include a burning sensation when urinating, a vaginal discharge or bleeding between periods.

Rectal infection causes painful bowel movements, anal itching, discharge or bleeding, while throat infections are mild and may result in a sore throat.

Eighty percent of women and 15 percent of men have no symptoms.

Chances of survival
Gonorrhea can be fatal when it spreads to the blood or joints. Untreated gonorrhea can cause other serious complications. In women it is a common cause of PID (see page 90), which can damage fallopian tubes, cause chronic pelvic pain and lead to internal abscesses that are difficult to treat. In men, gonorrhea can cause painful inflammation of the epididymis (in the testicles) that can lead to infertility.

How do I get rid of it?
A person is infectious until they have been treated. Treatment is with cephalosporin or quinalone type of antibiotics, but this is becoming more difficult as drug-resistant strains are on the increase.

What is it?
It is a rare but acute respiratory infection.

Where can I catch it?
The hantavirus is carried by white-footed mice, deer mice, cotton rats and rice rats in the United States. It is carried in the rodent saliva, urine and droppings and becomes airborne if infected materials are stirred up. Rarely, you can also become infected following a bite from an infected rodent, or by transferring infected material to your mouth by touching it or eating food that has been contaminated with rodent saliva, urine or droppings. Infection is particularly likely when cleaning, vacuuming or sweeping an area also inhabited by rodents. Infections most often occur in the autumn when small rodents move into our homes as the temperature drops.

Major outbreaks
The syndrome was first identified in 1993, and has since been traced back to 1959 and diagnosed in patients in over half the states in the United States.

How do I know I have it?
You will feel tired, feverish and ache, especially in your hips, thighs, back and shoulders. You may also vomit, suffer with diarrhea and have abdominal pain. You may begin to feel dizzy, and your head will ache. Up to 10 days later, you will begin coughing and will begin to fight for breath as your lungs fill with fluid.

Chances of survival
You currently have a 50 percent likelihood of surviving HPS. The syndrome can result in renal failure, pulmonary oedema and cardio-respiratory collapse.

How do I get rid of it?
As there is no specific drug treatment for HPS, the best chance of survival is to alert your physician early to having been close to rodents, as early hospitalisation is crucial. Patients are admitted to intensive care and treatment is supportive; intubation supports their breathing. Where physical activity is restricted, patients will make a better recovery.

What is it?
A disease caused by too much iron in body tissues.

Where can I catch it?
The majority of cases of hemochromatosis are hereditary, caused by the inheritance of a defect in a gene, called HFE, which helps to control how much iron your body absorbs from the food you consume. However, there are two other forms of hemochromatosis that are not caused by a faulty HFE gene, juvenile and neonatal hemochromatosis. Juvenile hemochromatosis involves a different gene, known as hemojuvelin. The causes of the neonatal form of the disease are unknown.

Major outbreaks
About one in 10 of the Caucasian population carries the faulty HFE gene and is at risk of developing hemochromatosis. Cases of non-hereditary forms of the disease are rare.

How do I know I have it?
Hereditary forms usually show first symptoms between 30 and 50 years of age in men, and over the age of 50 in women, although many people are asymptomatic when they are first diagnosed. Juvenile hemochromatosis will develop before the age of 30 years. You will have painful joints, feel lacking in energy, have a painful abdomen and a low sex drive and may develop heart problems and arthritis. Without early treatment, the iron will build up in your body tissues, leading to serious complications, such as cirrhosis of the liver, cancer of the liver or liver failure, pancreatic damage that may lead to diabetes, an irregular heart beat or heart failure, impotence, early menopause, greying or bronzing of the skin and thyroid problems.

Chances of survival
Juvenile and hereditary hemochromatosis can be fatal if left untreated. Neonatal is a severe disorder, and the baby is either stillborn or dies days after birth.

How do I get rid of it?
Doctors will remove about a pint of blood from your body once or twice a week. Once your iron levels have returned to normal, you will have to repeat the process about four times a year. If this is done before your organs have been damaged, you will prevent serious complications from developing.

HEPATITIS A

What is it?

A highly contagious viral infection of the liver caused by the hepatitis A virus (HAV), one of six strains of hepatitis viral infection, named A, B, C, D, E and G.

Where can I catch it?

The most common cause of infection with hepatitis A is from contaminated water or food, and close contact with an infected person. It is usually transmitted from fecal-oral contamination, where, for example, an infected person does not wash their hands sufficiently after using the toilet and before preparing food.

Major outbreaks

Hepatitis A is found commonly, with about one third of Americans having HAV antibodies, indicating that they have been exposed to the virus at some point.

How do I know I have it?

In some cases, people with a hepatitis A infection are asymptomatic. It is often misdiagnosed as intestinal flu (gastroenteritis), as symptoms are similar. You will feel tired, you'll lose your appetite, feel nauseous and will vomit. Your abdomen will be tender, especially on the right-hand side under your ribs. You may also develop jaundice that will make your skin and the whites of your eyes appear yellow. You will have muscle pain and may feel itchy.

Chances of survival

In most cases, the liver will be healed completely within a couple of months. Where patients are elderly or have other underlying medical conditions, the disease can be more serious. It can, in rare cases, lead to liver failure or contribute to the hardening of the arteries.

How do I get rid of it?

There is no specific treatment for hepatitis A, but you will need to ensure you maintain an adequate food and fluid intake so as to avoid any permanent damage to your liver.

What is it?
A serious viral infection of the liver caused by the hepatitis B virus (HBV).

Where can I catch it?
HBV is contracted in the same way as HIV, via the blood or body fluids of someone who is infected with the virus during unprotected sex, or needle sharing.

Major outbreaks
More than 1.25 million Americans have a chronic hepatitis B infection.

How do I know I have it?
You will lose your appetite, feel nauseous and begin vomiting about six weeks after exposure to the virus. You will feel tired and have abdominal pain around the area of your liver (the right-hand side under your ribs). You will have joint pain, and your skin and the whites of your eyes may turn yellow, as you become jaundiced.

Chances of survival
Most adults have an acute form of the virus, lasting about six months before being cleared from the body by your immune system. This leads to a full recovery. Infants and children with hepatitis B don't do so well, with almost 90 percent of infants and 50 percent of children under five years developing the chronic form of the disease, which can last decades without detection before finally causing serious liver damage. Serious complications can develop from chronic hepatitis B, including cirrhosis, a permanent scarring of the liver. Approximately 5,000 die in the United States every year from hepatitis B related causes.

How do I get rid of it?
If you know you have been exposed to hepatitis B, you can receive an injection of hepatitis B immune globulin within the first 24 hours after exposure. This may prevent you from becoming infected. Chronic hepatitis B may be treated with antiviral drugs, such as interferon. If the infection causes severe liver damage, transplantation may be recommended.

What is it?
A fungal lung disease caused by the fungus *Histoplasmosis capsultum*.

Where can I catch it?
The fungus is found growing throughout the world, thriving in soil that contains bird or bat droppings. Its spores are light enough to float in the air and can then be inhaled, where they will enter your lungs and become attached to the lining. School-aged children and elderly men are the most common victims of histoplasmosis.

Major outbreaks
Histoplasmosis used to be considered rare, with only 71 cases identified in the United States before 1945. In areas where the *Histoplasmosis capsultum* fungus is common, up to 80 percent of the population will test positive for having been exposed to the infection. An estimated 50 million North Americans will have been infected.

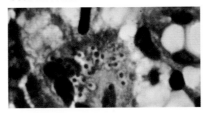

How do I know I have it?
In most cases, you will not know you have inhaled the spores, as the infection is often asymptomatic. If you contract a milder form of the disease, it will not last long, and you will have a fever, a cough, and chest pain and feel generally unwell, as with a mild dose of the flu. If you have an already weakened immune system, for example because of AIDS, leukemia or organ transplant, you may develop a chronic form of the disease, where the infection affects areas of your body besides your lungs. You may develop anemia, hepatitis or meningitis. In people with underlying respiratory conditions, such as emphysema, you may develop a TB-like disease.

Chances of survival
There are very few fatalities caused by histoplasmosis. Most cases result in full recovery.

How do I get rid of it?
The milder forms of histoplasmosis will not need treatment. In more severe cases, you will be hospitalised for several weeks and given daily injections of a drug called Amphotericin B.

What is it?
A virus that weakens the immune system and that can cause AIDS.

Where can I catch it?
You are at risk of becoming infected with HIV if your broken skin or mucous membranes (the moist, thin tissues in some of the body's openings, such as the vagina, the mouth, the rectum and the opening of the penis) come into direct contact with the infected blood, semen or vaginal secretions of another person. In simple terms, you are at risk of contracting the HIV virus if you have unprotected sex, vaginal, oral or anal, or if you are an intravenous drug user and you share needles. Accidental needle pricks carry a low risk of infection. A woman can transfer the virus to her baby during pregnancy, in labour or whilst breastfeeding, although the risks are greatly reduced if the woman receives treatment during these periods.

Major outbreaks
The first known case of HIV infection was in 1959, when the virus was seen in the blood sample of a man in the Democratic Republic of the Congo. It was seen in the United States from the mid-1970s, and by the 1980s the term AIDS was being used to describe the collection of diseases associated with this viral infection. In 1983 the HIV virus was identified as the virus that causes AIDS.

Since this time, AIDS has become a worldwide epidemic, with more than 38 million people living with HIV, with figures still rising.

How do I know I have it?
You will probably not notice that you have been infected with HIV, as there may be no symptoms at all at first, but more commonly a flu-like illness occurs briefly up to six weeks after becoming infected. You may now remain asymptomatic for as long as nine years or more, but all this time the virus is growing in your lymph nodes and begins to attack the white blood cells (T-cells) that are the frontline of your immune system. At some point you will begin to develop mild symptoms, such as swollen lymph nodes, diarrhea, weight loss, a fever, a cough and shortness of breath.

After 10 years or more, the last phase of HIV infection begins, which may include symptoms severe enough for the infection to be redefined as AIDS, in which case your immune system will be so weak as to leave you vulnerable to opportunistic infections, such as a type of pneumonia known as PCP (*Pneumocystis carinii*).

The symptoms you will experience during the late stages of HIV infection will leave you with chronic fatigue, night sweats and feverish chills with a temperature higher than 38°C (100°F) that last for several weeks. Your lymph nodes will swell and remain swollen for at least 12 weeks, and you will suffer with a persistent headache and chronic diarrhea.

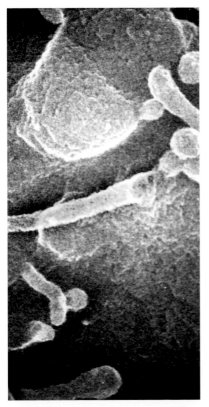

Chances of survival

Powerful new drug treatments, which have been available since 1996, are significantly changing predictions about how many HIV positive people will develop AIDS and how quickly they will develop it, so that it is not possible to make accurate assessments. It is certainly a very different picture than established thinking before 1996, when it was believed about half of HIV infected individuals would develop AIDS within 10 years or so. If HIV infection does progress to AIDS, it remains a terminal condition.

How do I get rid of it?

Treatment focuses on suppressing symptoms for as long as possible, and is known as highly active antiretroviral therapy (HAART). HAART will bring levels of the virus in your body down to very low levels, but it cannot cure you of the virus.

IRRITABLE BOWEL SYNDROME (IBS)

What is it?
A disorder of the large intestine, or colon, which changes the way the colon works, making it less effective and causing discomfort for sufferers.

Where can I catch it?
IBS occurs all over the world, but especially in the United States, Europe and New Zealand. There is no known cause of IBS, although many possible causes have been considered. There is no evidence to implicate genetics, diet, hormones or infection as the underlying cause.

Major outbreaks
IBS affects about 20 percent of the population, and twice as many women as men. It is usually diagnosed between the ages of 20 and 40, although many sufferers trace their symptoms back to childhood. Exact figures are not possible, as it is believed that as many as three quarters of sufferers will not report their symptoms to a doctor.

How do I know I have it?
There are many symptoms associated with IBS that can also indicate other disorders. A doctor will be looking for you to have suffered the following symptoms for a total of three months of the year: stomach pains that ease off after defecation and a change in how frequently you defecate (less than three times a week or more than three times a day). In addition you may notice your stools becoming harder or looser, you may pass mucus or feel bloated.

Chances of survival
IBS is not life-threatening and does not cause long-term damage to the intestine nor develop into more serious conditions such as cancer. However, in some cases, it can become a disabling condition, affecting a person's ability to work, travel and socialise.

How do I get rid of it?
It is not possible to get rid of IBS, but medication usually helps manage it. Fiber supplements and laxatives will be prescribed for constipation. You may be prescribed antidepressants and tranquilisers, as there is some evidence to suggest that stress can heighten the symptoms. Careful attention to your diet will be important, ensuring that you include enough fiber and wholegrain foods, drinking six to eight glasses of water, avoiding carbonated drinks and gum, as they create gas. Eating slowly and avoiding large meals will also reduce the discomfort you experience. Exercise and stress management are also beneficial.

What is it?
A virus carried by mosquitoes that affects the central nervous system.

Where can I catch it?
Japanese encephalitis is carried in the summer and autumn in rural areas of many Asian countries including specifically, Japan, China, Taiwan, Thailand and Korea by the mosquito, *Culex tritaeniorhynchus*.

Major outbreaks
There are up to 50,000 cases a year of Japanese encephalitis reported in Asia, although very few cases of travellers to the regions developing the illness (fewer than one person a year in the United States). Japan, China, Taiwan, Thailand and Korea have had major epidemics in the past, but vaccination has now brought the disease under control.

How do I know I have it?
If you escape with a mild infection, you will suffer nothing more than a headache and a raised temperature. If you develop a high fever, a stiff neck and feel lethargic and disorientated, your infection is more severe. You may go on to suffer tremors and convulsions, fall into a coma or experience spastic paralysis, where your limbs contract and become immobile.

Chances of survival
Thirty percent of people who contract Japanese encephalitis will die, and a further 30 percent will be left with brain damage and paralysis.

How do I get rid of it?
There is no treatment or specific anti-viral drug that is effective in treating Japanese encephalitis.

KAWASAKI SYNDROME

What is it?
A rare inflammatory disease that can affect the heart, skin and circulatory and immune systems.

Where can I catch it?
The disease is predominantly a childhood condition, most commonly found in Japan and in children of Japanese ethnicity living around the world, although it affects all ethnic groups. The precise cause is unknown, although some professionals speculate that it is an allergic reaction, triggered by other infections. Eighty percent of patients diagnosed with Kawasaki syndrome are children under the age of five years. You are twice as likely to catch Kawasaki syndrome as a boy.

How do I know I have it?
You will develop a sudden and raging fever, as high as 40ºC (104ºF), which can last for anything from five to 14 days, and it will not respond to either Ibuprofen or antibiotics. Your chest and genital area will become covered in a rash, and as the fever subsides, your skin will begin to peel, firstly at your finger tips and toenails, then the palms of your hands, the soles of your feet and your genital area. Your lips will appear bright red and will crack, and your tongue will have a thick white coating and will be covered with prominent red 'strawberry-like' bumps. Your palms, soles, eyelids and eyeballs will be swollen and dark, purplish-red, and the lymph glands in your neck may also swell. These symptoms can last for three months.

Chances of survival
Kawasaki syndrome is fatal in two percent of cases, mostly as a result of heart attack. One third of patients develop complications including pneumonia, diarrhea, jaundice, meningitis, hepatitis (an inflamed liver) and arthritis. The disease can affect the heart and circulatory system, causing the heart to swell (myocarditis), an irregular heartbeat (arrhythmia) or the thinning of the wall of the coronary arteries (aneurysm).

Major outbreaks
Kawasaki syndrome usually affects individual children, but there are documented incidents of small epidemics breaking out. In the United States there are over 4,000 children a year hospitalised with diagnosed Kawasaki syndrome.

A few patients will also develop gangrene in their hands or feet. In the United States, Kawasaki syndrome remains the major cause of pediatric-acquired heart disease.

How do I get rid of it?

Early hospitalisation is vital if you are to increase your chances of survival without complications. You will be given a drip containing a product called gamma globulin, which has antibodies that help protect your heart from the effects of the syndrome. Aspirin is also given, often for several months. Your heart and lungs will be monitored with chest X-rays, ECGs and ultrasound scans. If heart complications do occur, they can affect your life expectancy and can cause death from heart attack as much as 10 years later.

What is it?
An acute animal-borne viral disease, first isolated in Lassa, Nigeria, in 1969 when two missionary nurses died from the virus.

Where can I catch it?
The disease is transferred to humans from infected Mastomys rats, either by direct contact with droppings or urine or by inhalation of droplets of infected rodent excretions in the air. The disease also passes from person to person.

Major outbreaks
Lassa fever is endemic in Western Africa, specifically Sierra Leone, Nigeria, Ghana and Liberia, with an estimated 300,000 cases a year. In some areas hospital admissions suggest that up to 16 percent of the populations of these areas could have Lassa fever at any one time.

How do I know I have it?
In 80 percent of cases, the disease is mild or asymptomatic. You may have fever, sore throat, headaches and a cough. You may also be nauseous, have diarrhea, muscle, chest and abdominal pain. You may develop swelling in your throat and eyes, and as the symptoms subside, you may lose your hair and your co-ordination.

If you develop a more severe form of the disease, you may hemorrhage, have seizures and develop encephalopathy (brain dysfunction) or hearing loss. You will go into shock, your lungs will fill with fluid and your face and neck may swell.

Chances of survival
Up to 20 percent of patients who are hospitalised with Lassa fever will die, and the disease is worse for women in the final three months of pregnancy. About 95 percent of fetuses will die in the wombs of infected mothers. Overall, however, survival rates are far greater, with only one percent of all cases of Lassa fever resulting in death.

Deafness affects one third of Lassa fever patients, of whom many will have permanent hearing loss.

How do I get rid of it?
The anti-viral drug Ribavarin is effective in treating Lassa fever if administered early.

What is it?

A severe infection caused by the bacterium *Legionella pneumophila*, which was first traced following an outbreak of pneumonia in 221 of the delegates at a 1976 American Legion convention in Philadelphia. Most of the 43 ex-service personnel that died were Legionnaires.

Where can I catch it?

The bacterium that causes Legionnaires' disease is found in warm water and infects people who inhale tiny airborne droplets, for example from hot water systems and domestic air coolers. There is speculation that the bacterium can also infect a person who drinks contaminated water

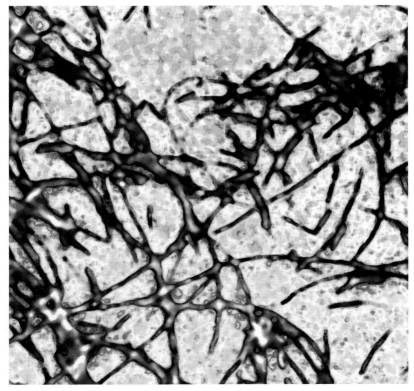

or who has open wounds and comes into contact with contaminated water. People with low immunity, as a result of HIV, organ transplant or chemotherapy, for example, are at much greater risk of contracted the disease. Smokers, heavy drinkers, diabetics and those over the age of 65 are also more likely to contract Legionnaires'.

Major outbreaks

Legionnaires' is often considered to be a rare disease, but this is not the case. Estimated figures for the United States alone indicate up to 100,000 cases of Legionnaires' a year. However, few cases are publicised, and unless special laboratory tests are carried out, a case of pneumonia will not be identified as Legionnaires' at all; hence there is much under-diagnosis. Outbreaks affecting lots of people at once are well covered in the media, but as much as 80 percent of cases in the United States and the United Kingdom are isolated, where only one or two people at a time develop the disease.

How do I know I have it?

You will feel lethargic, nauseous and have a headache. Your muscles will ache, you will have a dry cough and chest pain and you will be highly feverish. As the disease progresses, most patients develop

pneumonia, where some of the air sacs in the lungs fill with fluid. You may become confused or hallucinate, and other body functions may be affected, for example your kidneys and even your mental functions.

Chances of survival

Up to 15 percent of known cases of Legionnaires' disease result in fatalities.

How do I get rid of it?

You will be treated with antibiotics, Eryhtromycin and Azithromycin, which are most effective where cases are caught early. Hospitalisation is usually required, especially if you develop pneumonia in both lungs.

What is it?

A parasitic disease spread by the bite of infected sand flies, which themselves become infected by biting an infected animal or human. There are several forms, but the three most common are cutaneous (CL), mucocutaneous (MCL) and, the most severe form, visceral (VL).

Where can I catch it?

It is most common in rural areas and is found in about 88 countries, mostly in the tropics and subtropics, where approximately 350 million people are at risk of contracting the disease. It occurs in China, the Middle East, south central Asia, the Mediterranean basin, southern regions of the former Soviet Union, Africa (particularly East and North), Texas, Mexico and Central and South America.

Sand flies are at their most active dusk and during the evening, but they will also bite during the day if disturbed. They are about one-third the size of mosquitoes, and they do not buzz, so they can be hard to detect. A single bite can transmit the disease.

Major outbreaks

More than 90 percent of the world's cases of VL are in India, Bangladesh, Nepal, Sudan and Brazil.

There are over two million new cases each year, of which about 1.5 million are CL and 500,000 are VL.

How do I know I have it?

If you have CL you will develop several skin sores a few weeks after becoming infected. These ulcers usually end up looking like little volcanoes and will last months or years if untreated.

With MCL you will develop CL-type lesions of which some will appear in your nose, mouth and throat and will cause serious disfigurement if untreated.

VL will make you chronically sick within several months of becoming infected, and it attacks internal organs such as the liver, spleen and bone marrow. You will also suffer from fever, weight loss, anemia and swollen glands.

Chances of survival

If not treated, VL is fatal in 95 percent of cases.

How do I get rid of it?

CL will heal on its own, but will take months, even years, and leave ugly scars. MCL and VL require urgent treatment with Pentostam or Glucantime.

LEPROSY
(Hansen's Disease)

What is it?

A chronic, though slow-growing, mildly infectious disease caused by a bacillus, *Mycobacterium leprae*. It affects the skin, nerves and mucous membranes. The bacillus was discovered by Norwegian Dr. Armauer Hansen in 1873, although this ancient disease's first written mention is dated 600 BC.

Where can I catch it?

It is most common in warm, wet areas in the tropics and subtropics. It is thought to be transmitted through breathing in the airborne water droplets that shoot out of an infected person's nose and throat when they cough or sneeze. However, despite its bad press, leprosy is not very contagious; about 95 percent of people have natural immunity to the disease.

A person with leprosy who has been receiving medication for at least two weeks is not contagious.

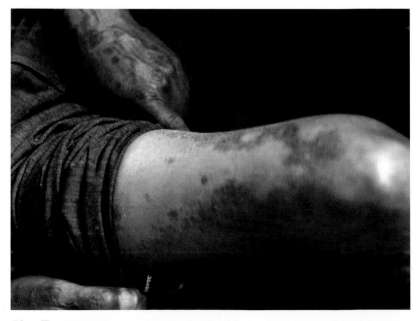

Major outbreaks
In the 1980s over 12 million people were affected. Now only about one million people have leprosy and a further 750,000 are infected each year. In 2002 the WHO said that Brazil, Madagascar, Mozambique, Tanzania and Nepal had 90 percent of all cases.

How do I know I have it?
The disease progresses very slowly, and symptoms can take up to 20 years to appear. The first sign is a spot on the skin that loses feeling and appears either lighter or darker than the surrounding skin. If you develop less than five of these patches you are suffering from paucibacillary (PB) leprosy; more than five is called multibacillary (MB) leprosy.

Without treatment your hands and feet become numb and you will be more susceptible to injuries (such as cuts or burns) because of your loss of pain warnings; these may develop into serious infections such as gangrene. If the nerves around your eyes are affected, you may lose sensation in your eye and the blinking reflex, leading to eye damage and blindness. The internal lining of your nose may disintegrate and ultimately collapse.

Chances of survival
Leprosy is not fatal, but for centuries it has caused its sufferers to be shunned and expelled from society.

How do I get rid of it?
Its progress can be completely halted with a course of three antibiotics: dapsone, rifampin and clofazimine. Treatment may last up to two years.

What is it?
A bacterial illness caused by *Leptospira interrogans*, a corkscrew-shaped micro-organism. It is a potentially serious illness that can afflict many body parts.

Where can I catch it?
Humans catch leptospirosis from water (swimming or drinking), soil or vegetation that has been contaminated by the urine of infected animals (most commonly rodents). The bacteria can be swallowed or can enter the body through broken skin or mucous membranes (nose, throat). It is even possible to catch it while canoeing or wading through contaminated water.

Major outbreaks
It is found worldwide, but it is most common in the tropics, where heavy rainfall and flooding help to spread the bacteria. In 1995 an epidemic affected over 2,000 people and led to 13 deaths in Nicaragua after heavy flooding. The disease also occurs in cities with a large population of infected rats.

How do I know I have it?
Symptoms appear about 10 days after infection (although they may take up to a month) and include headache, fever, nausea, vomiting, muscle aches and jaundice (yellow skin and eyes). A special blood test will confirm infection.

Chances of survival
Without antibiotic treatment leptospirosis can damage the liver and lead to meningitis, kidney failure, internal bleeding and death. With treatment the illness lasts from between a few days and a month.

How do I get rid of it?
Leptospirosis is treated with antibiotics such as doxycycline or penicillin, which should be given early to be effective. Serious cases may require intravenous antibiotics.

What is it?

An illness caused by infection with a bacterium, *Borrelia burgdorferi*. It is named after the town of Lyme, Connecticut, where it was first discovered in 1975.

Where can I catch it?

It is spread to humans through the bite of an infected tick. The bite is painless, so it can suck your blood without you knowing. The ticks become infected by biting small rodents or deer that harbour the bacteria in their blood systems and tissues.

The ticks are found in grassy areas (including lawns) and in woodland sites, even during the milder part of winter.

Major outbreaks

It is found worldwide and throughout the United States, mostly in New York, Massachusetts, Connecticut, Rhode Island and New Jersey.

How do I know I have it?

Between three days and two weeks after infection, many people develop a red bull's-eye rash that slowly spreads outwards like an expanding red ring from the central bite point. This is accompanied by flu-like symptoms such as fever, headache, tiredness, muscle aches and joint pain. However, some people show no symptoms, while others develop the flu-like symptoms without the rash.

Chances of survival

It is easy to ignore earlier symptoms if they are mild, but after several months without treatment, some people develop arthritis, aseptic meningitis, Bell's palsy (see page 20) and encephalitis (inflammation of the brain) and in rare cases even heart problems such as myopericarditis (inflammation of the tissues surrounding the heart), a blockage or enlarged heart. It can also give you eye, lung and digestive problems.

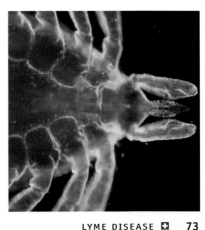

How do I get rid of it?
Doxycycline or amoxicillin are the drugs of choice and are effective if used early on. More serious cases require a month's treatment of intravenous ceftriaxone or penicillin.

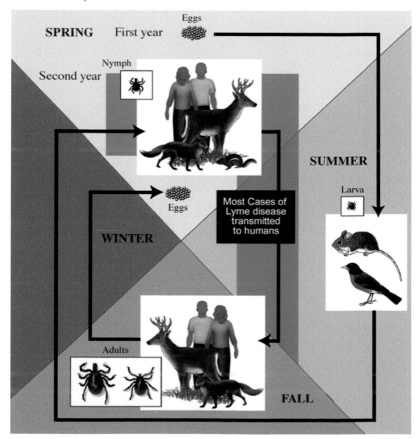

Eggs

SPRING   First year

Nymph

Second year

SUMMER

Larva

Most Cases of Lyme disease transmitted to humans

Eggs

WINTER

Adults

FALL

What is it?

A parasitic disease transmitted from person to person by the bite of infected female Anopheles mosquitoes. It results in fever, chills and anemia. The parasites are called Plasmodium; there are four species, one of which, *Plasmodium falciparum*, is potentially fatal. The parasites infect the liver where they develop and then attack the red blood cells.

Where can I catch it?

Malaria is very common worldwide, especially in tropical and subtropical countries and large areas of Central and South America, sub-Saharan Africa, the Indian subcontinent, Southeast Asia, the Middle East and Oceania. There are between 300 and 500 million cases of malaria each year, and it kills more than one million people.

You can catch it from a blood transfusion from infected blood, and a mother can also pass it to her unborn baby.

Major outbreaks

While it is a significant problem in over 90 countries, more than 90 percent of cases occur in sub-Saharan Africa, where it kills a child every 30 seconds. The WHO says 'In absolute numbers, malaria kills 3,000 children per day under five years of age. It is a death toll that far exceeds the [child] mortality rate from AIDS.'

How do I know I have it?

You would normally show symptoms between 10 days to four weeks after infection, but in some cases they may take up to a year. These include cycles of chills and fever that recur every two or three days. While the parasites attack the red blood cells, you will feel very hot and nauseous; when the cells eventually rupture and the parasites burst out to infect more cells, you feel very cold and will suffer extreme shaking chills. You may also develop anemia and jaundice.

Chances of survival

With treatment, your chances of recovery are very good, but if you are infected with *Plasmodium falciparum* and treatment is delayed, you may develop meningitis or a ruptured spleen and a massive internal hemorrhage, liver and kidney failure.

How do I get rid of it?

The most frequently used medication is chloroquine; if the parasite is resistant to chloroquine, then qinidine, quinine, pyrimethamine and sulfadoxine may be used.

MARBURG HEMORRHAGIC FEVER

What is it?
A rare viral infection caused by a member of the Filoviridae family of viruses, as is the Ebola virus; named 'Marburg' after the German town where the first cases appeared.

Where can I catch it?
The virus affects monkeys and other primates and can be spread to humans directly following contact with an infected primate, in particular with their fluids or cell cultures in a laboratory environment. The virus will also spread from person to person, in droplets of body fluids or where there is direct contact with contaminated surfaces, objects or people.

Major outbreaks
The first outbreak of Marburg hemorrhagic fever was in 1967 in laboratories in Marburg and Frankfurt, Germany, as well as in Belgrade in the former Yugoslavia. Laboratory workers and medical personnel contracted the disease, totalling 37 people. The disease had spread to Europe in the form of infected monkeys, or their tissues, from Uganda. There have been a few quite isolated cases of the disease in each decade since that time in South Africa, Kenya and in the Congo.

How do I know I have it?
You will have a fever and chills, a headache and general muscle ache. After about five days, a rash will appear over your trunk, and you will feel nauseous, begin to vomit and develop diarrhea. Your throat will be sore and you will have stomach pain. At this point your symptoms could become more severe, with jaundice, an inflamed pancreas, marked weight loss, liver failure and massive hemorrhaging. The disease may affect several organs and you may go into shock and become delirious.

Chances of survival
About a quarter of all cases result in death, and for those that survive, recovery is a very long process, hampered by recurring bouts of hepatitis, or inflammation of the testes, spinal cord or eyes.

How do I get rid of it?
There is no specific treatment for this disease, but you will be hospitalised and supported with blood transfusions and intravenous fluids and your blood oxygen levels will be maintained.

What is it?

Inflammation of the meninges (the brain lining) caused by an infection of the spinal cord and the fluid that surrounds the brain. It is caused by either bacteria or a virus, depending on which type you have. Viral meningitis (caused by enteroviruses, such as coxsackieviruses and echoviruses) is usually quite mild, but bacterial meningitis (caused by *Hemophilus influenzae* type b, *Neisseria meningitidis* or *Streptococcus pneumoniae* bacteria) is very serious.

Where can I catch it?

Meningitis is found worldwide. The bacteria may live harmlessly in your mouth or throat, but sometimes they beat the body's immune system and enter the spinal fluid and begin to multiply. Both the bacteria and virus can be passed on through contact with the body fluids of an infected person (nasal mucus, saliva, etc.), which may be airborne or on objects.

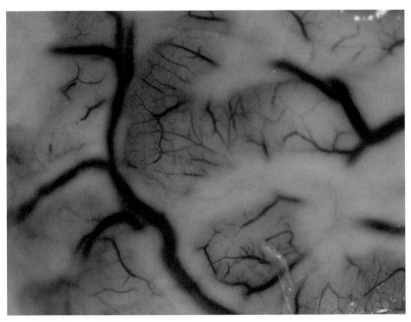

Major outbreaks

In Africa there are regular epidemics of bacterial meningitis. In 1996 an estimated 250,000 people were affected in West Africa and 25,000 died.

How do I know I have it?

The classic signs of both forms of meningitis are a fever, headache and a stiff neck, but other symptoms include light sensitivity, nausea, confusion and sleepiness. These symptoms may develop in just a few hours or over a couple of days.

Bacterial meningitis may cause septicemia (blood poisoning), in which case a pinprick rash appears under the skin. These spots do not turn white when pressed and without treatment they grow bigger and resemble fresh bruises (since subcutaneous bleeding is taking place).

You will need a spinal tap (when a needle is stuck into your spinal canal to remove fluid) so that a proper diagnosis can be made.

Chances of survival

Viral meningitis is usually quite mild (and rarely fatal), so you should recover within a few weeks, without specific treatment.

Bacterial meningitis often results in serious disability (e.g., deafness and brain damage) and death if it isn't treated early and aggressively.

How do I get rid of it?

Bacterial meningitis can be treated effectively with antibiotics, so long as it is treated early.

What is it?
It is a bacterium that is found in up to 30 percent of healthy people and lives in their noses and on their skin. Methicillin is an antibiotic, so MRSA is antibiotic resistant, making it potentially very dangerous to those with weakened immune systems.

Where can I catch it?
MRSA can be caught anywhere, but it is most often associated with hospitals. MRSA isn't dangerous in the ordinary environment, but it is a recurrent problem in hospitals where vulnerable patients who are exposed to the bacterium can become very sick, especially if it enters the body through a break in the skin or wound. Since so many people can be carriers, the bacterium may be spread through sneezing or via skin-to-skin contact, and it can also survive on surfaces such as linen, sinks, floors and even cleaning utensils.

Major outbreaks
So far there are 17 strains of MRSA that have been identified, of which strains 15 and 16 account for nearly all of MRSA bloodstream infections in the United Kingdom, and they are spreading to other countries. Some strains of MRSA are very successful at spreading between patients and even between hospitals. These strains are known as 'endemic' (or EMRSA).

Some people believe we are in the early stages of a situation where soon doctors will be powerless against some bacterial infections, after more than a century of antibiotic control and overuse.

How do I know I have it?
In a healthy person, there may be no symptoms, or just a mild throat infection. More serious symptoms depend on which part of the body has been infected, and they often result in swelling and tenderness at the infected site.

The only way to confirm infection is to take swabs and blood or urine samples, and send them to the laboratory for testing.

Chances of survival
If you are otherwise healthy, your chance of dying is minimal. If you are old or weak, your recovery will take longer.

How do I get rid of it?

As soon as you are diagnosed, you will be subjected to contact isolation, which means that everyone who comes into contact with you or anything you have touched must wash their hands, and you will usually be placed in your own room or in an isolation unit. Although MRSA is resistant to many antibiotics, most strains respond to the antibiotics vancomycin and teicoplanin, which must be given by injection or slowly through a drip. However, there are some strains of MRSA that are resistant even to these.

What is it?
A viral disease that is similar to smallpox, but much milder. It was first discovered in monkeys in a Danish zoo in the 1950s, but it has since been confirmed that it is only endemic to Central Africa. Many species of primates can catch monkeypox, and the virus has also been found in squirrels and rodents. The first reported human case was in 1970.

Where can I catch it?
It is spread either from a bite from an infected animal, contact with body fluids (blood, saliva, nasal mucus) or through small cuts or lesions on your skin. The virus may also contaminate objects such as clothing or bedding.

Major outbreaks
The largest recorded outbreak occurred in the former Zaire with over 500 people infected since February 1996, of which 85 percent were children age 16 and under. The first outbreak in the United States occurred in June 2003, transmitted from pet prairie dogs.

How do I know I have it?
The symptoms are similar to smallpox (see page 117). About 12 days after

infection you will suffer from a fever, tiredness, a headache, muscle aches and swollen lymph nodes (not a symptom of smallpox). A few days after the fever you will develop a rash, which usually starts on the face and spreads to anywhere else on your body. The spots fill with pus, then scab over and drop off.

Chances of survival
The illness lasts for up to a month. In Africa it has killed up to 10 percent of people who contract it, but in developed countries the risk is much lower because of better nutrition and healthcare.

How do I get rid of it?
There is no treatment for the illness, which lasts for up to a month. If you have had a smallpox vaccination you are at less risk of catching monkeypox in the first place.

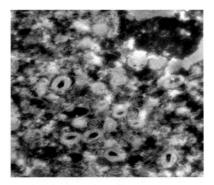

MUCORMYCOSIS

What is it?
A fungal infection, also known as zygomycosis, which affects the sinuses, brain or lungs. It is caused by the *Phycomycete* fungi, first described in 1885.

Where can I catch it?
The fungal spores are very common in soil worldwide and enter the body through the mouth and nose. People with a healthy immune system will not develop the disease, but those with compromised immunity are at greatest risk.

Major outbreaks
Although the spores are ubiquitous, the disease itself is rare, so outbreaks as such do not occur. The majority of reported cases have been in poorly controlled diabetics.

How do I know I have it?
Common symptoms include facial pain and swelling, sinusitis, headache, fever, nasal discharge and visual problems. Serious complications include blood clots in the brain, pneumonia and kidney infection. Black discoloration in the nose or on the palate is a clear indicator of infection.

Chances of survival
Even with treatment the death rate is very high. Early aggressive treatment is paramount and disfiguring surgery is often necessary.

How do I get rid of it?
The primary disease (such as diabetes) must be brought under control, while surgery to remove dead and infected tissue is essential. This may involve removal of the palate, and parts of the nose and eyes. Also treatment with high doses of intravenous antifungal drugs, such as amphotericin B, may be necessary.

What is it?

A subcutaneous bacterial infection caused by group A strep bacteria (the same one that causes strep throat). It destroys soft tissue, giving it the reputation as a 'flesh-eating' bacteria.

Where can I catch it?

It occurs when the A strep bacteria enter the body through a break in the skin. This can be anything from a wound to a paper cut or even a pinprick. Up to 30 percent of the population carry the bacteria in their throat or on the skin, without showing any symptoms. But when a carrier coughs or sneezes in the vicinity of a person with a wound or cut, the bacteria may be carried in the air by water droplets or transferred from the hands.

Major outbreaks

There are about 2,000 cases each year worldwide. By contrast, there are millions of cases of strep throat each year, so necrotizing fasciitis is very rare.

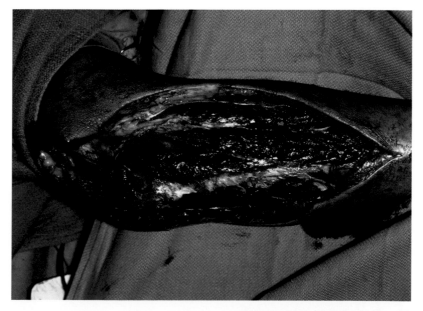

How do I know I have it?

Early signs include pain and swelling
in the area of the cut or wound that is
disproportionate to the injury. Initially
it may feel like a pulled muscle and
become more painful. Then flu-like
symptoms develop, including dizziness,
confusion, nausea and, as the body
becomes dehydrated, intense thirst.
Within three to four days the area of
infection swells and may have a purple
rash. Large dark patches appear that
become blisters filled with dark fluid.

Chances of survival

Without treatment blood pressure
drops severely and the body will go
into toxic shock, and loss of the affected
limb is a great risk. About 20 percent of
people with Necrotizing Fasciitis die. If
you are lucky, you will be left with minimal
scarring, but prompt diagnosis is vital
to minimise tissue damage.

How do I get rid of it?

You must receive hospital treatment
with intravenous antibiotics, and
removal of necrotic tissue. Hyperbaric
oxygen therapy (placing the person in
an oxygen saturated chamber at
increased pressure) also helps to
kill the bacteria.

ONCHOCERCIASIS
(River Blindness)

What is it?
An parasitic eye and skin disease caused by the prelarval (microfilaria) and adult stages of a microscopic worm, *Onchocerca volvulus*. It is transmitted to humans through the bite of an infected female blackfly, which are commonly found near rapidly flowing rivers and streams (hence the common name). It is the second leading infectious cause of blindness worldwide (number one is trachoma, see page 128).

Where can I catch it?
It is endemic in more than 25 countries, including Central Africa, the Arabian Peninsula, Mexico and South America. You need to receive several blackfly bites to become infected (unlike malaria, which takes just one). Blackflies bite during the day and are most common in remote African rural agricultural villages.

Major outbreaks
The WHO estimates that approximately 18 million people are infected worldwide (99 percent of whom live in Africa; about 270,000 are blind and 500,000 are visually impaired).

How do I know I have it?
Symptoms appear between nine to 24 months after infection, although it may be many years. These include a skin rash, eye lesions, lumps underneath the skin and unbearable itching. The eye lesions are very serious, as they can lead to blindness. The itching is so extreme that sufferers use knives and stones to scratch themselves; some have even been driven to suicide.

Chances of survival
Onchocerciasis is not fatal, but its effects can cause serious disability.

How do I get rid of it?
A drug called Ivermectin should be taken orally for several years. It kills the microfilaria, so it halts development of the disease, but it does not kill the adult parasites, which can live up to 15 years.

What is it?
It means literally 'porous bones'.
The inside of healthy bones is made
up of a dense mesh of protein, calcium
and other minerals. Osteoporosis occurs
when this structure becomes thinner and
weaker, resulting in a higher frequency
of broken bones, especially fractures to
the hips and wrist.

Where can I catch it?
Everyone is at risk as they grow
older and the rate of bone renewal
slows down. Factors that increase your
risk include, in women, a lack of the
hormone estrogen, early menopause or
hysterectomy and missing periods for
several months due to over-exercising
or excessive dieting. Men with low levels

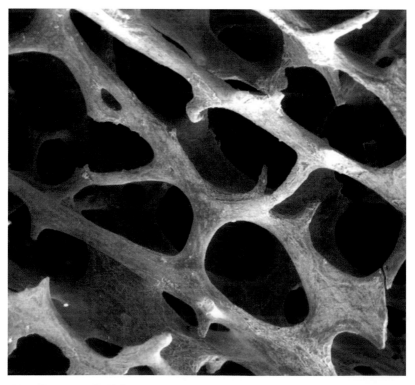

of the hormone testosterone are at greater risk. Inactivity, heavy drinking, smoking and a family history of osteoporosis are also significant risk factors.

Major outbreaks

Osteoporosis causes 1.5 million fractures in the United States alone each year. It affects half of women and a quarter of men over the age of 50.

How do I know I have it?

It is a silent disease. It drains away bone unnoticed for many years, and the first sign that anything is wrong is a broken limb after a minor bump or fall. An X-ray alone is not enough to measure bone density. You should have a dual energy X-ray absorptiometry (DXA) scan.

Chances of survival

Untreated osteoporosis is progressive and debilitating. Collapsing vertebrae can cause curvature of the spine and the so-called 'widow's hump', while a hip fracture can lead to permanent disability. Fortunately, there is a range of treatments available.

How do I get rid of it?

There is no cure, but early intervention can help to slow down the process of bone density loss. Treatment includes vitamin supplements and prescription drugs (such as fosamax and actonel) to increase bone mass, hormone replacement therapy for women and testosterone therapy for men. In our 40s and beyond bone density reduces faster than new bone can be manufactured, so the key to healthy bones longterm is to build up good bone mass early in life with a calcium-rich diet and plenty of weight-bearing exercise.

What is it?
Of the 16 species of parasitic flatworms (flukes) of the genus *Paragonimus* that infect humans, the most common is the oriental lung fluke known as *Paragonimus westermani*. It was discovered in a Bengal tiger living in a zoo in Holland by a keeper called Westerman. The adult fluke is reddish-brown, plump and oval, is about the size of a fingernail and it has suckers.

Where can I catch it?
The eggs hatch in water and develop in freshwater snails; then they move into crab or crayfish. Humans become infected with the cyst form of the parasite by eating these shellfish without cooking them properly, or by contaminating themselves or other food before they are cooked. Once they reach the small intestine the baby worms (metacercariae) leave their cysts, and many break through the intestinal and abdominal walls to enter the lungs, where they develop into adults after about six weeks. They can also enter other organs such as the brain, liver, kidney and spleen.

The adult flukes lay thousands of eggs inside the lungs. When they are coughed up or swallowed and passed in the stool the cycle begins again. Once infected you may cough up as many as 13,000 eggs each day.

Major outbreaks
Paragonimiasis is common throughout the Far East, West Africa, Asia, Indonesia, Papua New Guinea and South America. It is endemic in Korea, Japan, Taiwan, central China and the Philippines.

How do I know I have it?
Initially you may have diarrhea and abdominal pain followed by a mild fever, cough and chest pain. A few months later you will begin coughing up the eggs, and your sputum will be rusty coloured and may contain blood. Eventually, without treatment you may experience shortness of breath and will feel weak. Twenty-five percent of those infected show no symptoms.

Chances of survival
You may die during the acute phase of infection. If you survive you will recover spontaneously after a few months, but you may have recurrent symptoms for years. Complications include pneumonia and bronchitis, lung abscesses and empyema (a build up of blood or puss in a body cavity).

How do I get rid of it?

It can be treated with praziquantel or Bithionol, but surgery may be needed to remove the cysts. The flukes will die eventually, but without treatment this could take up to 20 years.

PELVIC INFLAMMATORY DISEASE (PID)

What is it?
An infection of the upper female genital tract that can affect the uterus, ovaries and fallopian tubes. It is the most common and serious complication of STDs, apart from AIDS.

Where can I catch it?
It is most commonly associated with chlamydia (see page 28) and gonorrhea (see page 54). It occurs when disease-causing bacteria migrates from the vagina and urethra to the upper genital tract. Symptoms of PID caused by gonorrhea often begin immediately after menstruation, and this may be because the cervical mucus plug that normally prevents the spread of infection is less effective at this time. Women are at greater risk of developing PID if they have STDs or have many different sexual partners. Also, the chances of developing PID increase after a previous episode.

Major outbreaks
It is the singlemost frequent serious infection in women. It affects over one million women in the United States alone each year, of whom the highest proportion are teenagers.

How do I know I have it?
The main symptoms of PID are lower abdominal pain and vaginal discharge. Other symptoms include fever, pain during intercourse and irregular menstrual bleeding. However, there may be no symptoms at all (especially in cases associated with chlamydia), which is especially dangerous, because severe damage may occur without the woman's knowledge.

It can be hard to diagnose even with a pelvic ultrasound, and it may be necessary for a doctor to perform a laparoscopy to confirm infection. This involves making a small incision below the naval and inserting a tiny viewing tube, which allows the doctor to see inside the abdomen and pelvic organs and take tissue samples for analysis.

Chances of survival
Without treatment it can lead to scarring, infertility, ectopic pregnancy, abscesses and chronic pelvic pain. More than 100,000 women in the United States become infertile as a result of PID each year. Severe cases require hospitalisation and even surgery.

How do I get rid of it?

Prompt treatment with two or more antibiotics is essential to minimise damage to reproductive organs. Also the woman's sexual partner should be treated to prevent re-infection.

What is it?
A disease initiated by bacterial infection causing severe inflammation and infection of the gums. It is the advanced stages of gum disease. The mild form of the disease is called gingivitis, but if this is untreated it will lead to periodontitis.

Where can I catch it?
Developing it is more a matter of 'how' rather than 'where'. It develops because of excessive build up of plaque and tartar because of poor dental hygiene, not brushing and flossing enough and not visiting the dentist to have tartar removed. The build up of bacteria damages and inflames the gums and spreads to the ligaments and bone that support the teeth. The body's immune system attacks healthy and diseased tissue alike in its attempt to combat bacterial attack. Smokers are up to seven times more likely to develop the disease, and diabetics have an increased risk of up to five times.

Major outbreaks
Because the early stages are painless, the American Dental Association reports that 75 percent of adults over the age of 35 have some form of periodontal disease (including gingivitis).

How do I know I have it?
If you are an adult whose teeth are loose and start to fall out, there's a good chance this is because of periodontitis, which is the main cause of tooth loss in adults. The gums will actually be quite painless and numb, unless you develop a tooth abscess. Your gums will be receded, red (or red-purple) and swollen, tender, bleed when brushed and appear shiny, plus you will have bad breath.

Chances of survival
It is not life-threatening, unless an infection from an abscess spreads into the bloodstream, although research has shown that people with periodontitis are more likely to suffer a heart attack, and a pregnant woman is more likely to give birth to a low-weight premature baby.

How do I get rid of it?
It is vital to seek immediate treatment from the dentist, who will give antibiotics, clean the teeth, remove build up of tartar and clean the pockets of infection that lie between the teeth and the gums. It may be necessary to remove some of the teeth so that decay doesn't spread to surrounding ones. In extreme cases bone grafting and surgery may be necessary.

What is it?

A highly contagious infection of the respiratory tract caused by *Bordetella pertussis* bacteria. It was first described in the 16th century and was a major cause of childhood mortality in developed countries during the 20th century.

Where can I catch it?

It occurs mostly in infants and young children. You can catch it by contact with the respiratory fluids and mucous of an infected person; this usually occurs when you breathe in the airborne water droplets that are expelled of an infected person's nose and throat when they cough or sneeze. You can also catch it from sharing utensils or cups with an infected person.

Major outbreaks

While it has been largely controlled in the industrialised countries through widespread vaccination (there are 5,000 to 7,000 cases each year in the United States), in developing countries there are about 30 million cases of pertussis and about 300,000 deaths each year.

How do I know I have it?

Between five and 21 days after infection you will experience cold-like symptoms such as a runny nose, sneezing, mild temperature and a cough. Within a fortnight the cough becomes much worse and you will suffer repeated coughing 'fits' with a characteristic 'whooping' sound as you try to catch your breath. The most unpleasant parts of the disease are difficulty in breathing during these attacks, and possible vomiting afterwards (due to lack of oxygen).

Chances of survival

Infants and young children often suffer major and sometimes fatal complications, including hypoxia (insufficient oxygen levels in blood and tissue), apnea (stopping breathing), pneumonia, inner ear infections, seizures, encephalopathy (brain disorders) and malnutrition.

How do I get rid of it?

It can be treated with antibiotics. An infected person remains contagious up to five days after treatment begins.

PLAGUE

What is it?

A bacterial disease caused by the bacterium *Yersinia pestis*, named after Alexandre Yersin, who first identified the bacillus in 1894 and developed an anti-serum to help fight the plague. It is carried among the rodent population by fleas.

Where can I catch it?

The fleas will feed from humans during periods of disease and high death rates in the rodent population. The plague can infect rabbits, squirrels, cats and dogs, and cats in particular can spread the disease directly to humans, as well as bringing fleas carrying the bacterium into the home. A bite from an infected flea causes bubonic plague. Inhalation of the bacillus following close contact with infected hosts will result in pneumonic plague, a form that bioterrorism experts fear, as it has one of the highest potentials for endangering public health of any potential biological weapon.

Major outbreaks

Over the centuries there is thought to have been over 200 million deaths caused by plague, and at least three pandemics, the most recent beginning in 1855 in China, which though controlled, is still ongoing. There are, on average, up to 2,000 new cases of plague worldwide reported every year, predominantly in Africa and Asia. The most recent outbreaks have been in India and Vietnam.

How do I know I have it?

If you contract bubonic plague, you will have very swollen tender lymph glands, called 'buboes', usually in your groin, armpits or neck. You will have feverish chills, a headache and feel extremely tired. Pneumonic plague will leave you with a very high fever, breathing difficulties and you will cough up blood.

Chances of survival

Bubonic plague results in death in up to 60 percent of untreated cases, and in up to 15 percent of treated cases. Pneumonic plague is far more deadly, and has 100 percent mortality rate where it is not treated in the first 24 hours.

How do I get rid of it?

As soon as you are diagnosed with suspected plague, you will be kept in isolation while the diagnosis is confirmed. You will be given antibiotics, in particular streptomycin or gentamycin.

What is it?

An ancient viral disease that damages the spine and nervous system and can lead to lower-limb paralysis. It gets its name from the Greek words 'polio' (grey) and 'myelon' (marrow, or spinal cord). It is caused by one of three enteroviruses of the *Picornaviridae* family that live in the intestinal tract, and it was categorized by Michael Underwood in 1789.

Where can I catch it?

The virus lives in the throat and intestinal tract of infected people and is present in their stools, which can be passed to others through poor hygiene and inadequate hand washing. It is not thought to spread by contaminating food and water, but it enters the body through the mouth.

Major outbreaks

Before mass immunisation in developed countries, polio was common (for example, at its peak in 1952 in the United States, there were 21,000 cases of paralysis due to polio infection). Now developing countries are at greatest risk, especially the Indian subcontinent, Asia and Africa, although there are less than 1,000 cases worldwide each year.

How do I know I have it?

Symptoms appear between seven and 14 days after infection. Most cases of polio result in mild symptoms such as sore throat, fever, nausea, vomiting, stomach pain and muscle stiffness, but one in 200 cases of polio infection result in paralysis, which in some cases is permanent.

Chances of survival

Polio is only fatal in the minority of cases when the virus infects the brain to cause paralysis of the muscles that control swallowing and breathing.

How do I get rid of it?

There is no treatment for polio, but you will require expert and early medical treatment to mitigate the effects.

What is it?
A very rare amoebic infection caused by *Naegleria fowleri*, which causes inflammation of the lining of the brain and spinal cord. It is usually fatal.

Where can I catch it?
The amoeba is present worldwide and lives in soil and many lakes, ponds, rivers and under-chlorinated swimming pools. During warm weather the amoeba can multiply rapidly, increasing the chances of exposure, which is high, but actual infection is very low. The risk appears to be greatest during the hot summer months for those swimming in warm, shallow water, where bacteria are present in high numbers (the food source of the amoeba).

Infection occurs when the amoeba enters the body through the nose or mouth when a person is diving or swimming underwater. They then migrate up the nasal passage to the brain and spinal cord, where they multiply and cause brain and spinal cord swelling. It cannot be transmitted from person to person.

Major outbreaks
Since the disease was identified 25 years ago, fewer than 100 cases have been reported in the United States, as there are fewer than three infections each year, and these cases are always young healthy people who have been swimming in fresh water during the previous week.

How do I know I have it?
Between one to seven days after infection, following swimming in infected water, the onset of symptoms is rapid; they include fever, headache, nausea, vomiting, neck stiffness, photophobia, disorientation, seizures and coma. The symptoms are indistinguishable from acute bacterial meningitis.

Chances of survival
The disease is usually fatal within three to seven days.

How do I get rid of it?
Prompt diagnosis may allow treatment with very high doses of amphotericin B, but in most cases primary amoebic meningoencephalitis is only diagnosed after death. Only five people have survived the disease (that's about three percent of reported cases).

PSITTACOSIS

What is it?
An infection caused by the bacterium *Chlamydia psittaci*, which is primarily a disease of birds (affecting over 70 species) but sometimes spreads to humans. It is also known as Parrot disease, ornithosis and chlamydiosis. The word psittacosis is derived from the Greek word for parrot, *Psittakos*.

Where can I catch it?
The bacterium infect wild and domestic birds and poultry. Humans are infected by inhaling dried secretions from infected birds, such as feather dust, saliva and droppings. People most at risk are those who keep or work with pet birds such as parrots, parakeets, macaw and cockatiels and poultry, especially turkeys and ducks. Infected birds may appear listless, shivering and suffer weight loss and breathing difficulties. But they may have a latent form of the illness that has no symptoms. It is rare to catch the infection from another person.

Major outbreaks
It is present worldwide, but it is quite rare in humans, with less than 200 cases diagnosed per year in the United States.

How do I know I have it?
Symptoms can appear between one to four weeks after infection and include a rapid onset of fever and chills, muscle aches, rash, headache, photophobia (light sensitivity), shortness of breath, dry cough and bloody sputum.

Chances of survival
Fatal cases have been reported, and complications include endocarditis, hepatitis and neurological problems.

How do I get rid of it?
Antibiotic treatment with drugs such as tetracycline, doxycycline and erythromycin should lead to a full recovery.

What is it?

An infection spread by animals (especially cattle, sheep and goats, and occasionally domestic pets) caused by the bacteria *Coxiella burnetii*.

Where can I catch it?

It is present worldwide. The bacteria are found in the milk, urine and feces of infected animals and are also present in high numbers when an infected animal gives birth. They are very hardy and can survive outside their hosts for a long time, and they are resistant to heat and many disinfectants.

The most common way of humans becoming infected is by inhaling bacteria in the air. They can also be passed on in the unpasteurized milk of an infected animal and through tick bites. They rarely pass from human to human. Only a few bacteria are required for infection, and for this reason, it is a possible bioterrorism threat.

Major outbreaks

The disease occurs worldwide but reliable infection rates are difficult to assess, as the disease is underreported.

How do I know I have it?

Symptoms usually appear about two to three weeks after infection. Half of those infected have very mild symptoms, but the other half have more serious ones such as a high fever, severe headache, sore throat, confusion, coughing, vomiting and diarrhea, stomach pains and chest pains and are at high risk of developing pneumonia or hepatitis. The fever lasts up to two weeks, and most people recover without treatment and then often have lifelong immunity.

Chances of survival

Serious complications include inflammation of the lungs or heart and neurological problems, but only one to two percent of acute sufferers die of the disease.

How do I get rid of it?

Treatment with an antibiotic called Doxycycline is very effective if taken during the first three days of illness.

What is it?
A viral disease of mammals most often transmitted through the bite of a rabid animal. It's a very old disease and has its origin in Sanskrit, 3000 BC; 'rabhas' means 'to do violence'.

Where can I catch it?
Each year, it kills more than 50,000 people. Rabies is a big problem in Asia, Africa and Central and South America. In the United States, rabies has been reported in every state except Hawaii.

Most cases occur in wild animals like raccoons, skunks, bats and foxes. Rabies is passed on through saliva, and the most common way is through the bite of a rabid animal. Although domestic animals account for less than 10 percent of the reported rabies cases, over 90 percent of human infection is caused by a bite from a rabid (often stray) dog.

Major outbreaks
The first description of the disease dates from the 23rd century BC in the Eshuma Code of Babylon. In the 19th century, canine or street rabies was a scourge everywhere, especially in Europe. Nowadays the number of rabies-related human deaths in the United States has declined from more than 100 annually at the turn of the century to one or two per year in the 1990s.

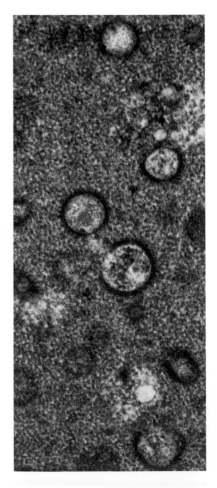

How do I know I have it?

In humans, symptoms usually develop one to three months after the bite. If you've developed symptoms, it's usually too late (only six people have survived clinical rabies).

Early symptoms include fever, headache, sore throat and fatigue. After the virus spreads to your brain, you'll feel anxious, confused and unable to sleep. You may also feel pain or tingling at the site of the bite, experience hallucinations, hydrophobia ('fear of water' due to spasms in the throat) and paralysis. A few days later you'll sink into a coma and die.

Chances of survival

Excellent, so long as you wash the bite and seek medical treatment.

How do I get rid of it?

The first anti-rabies treatment was discovered by Louis Pasteur in 1885, when he used the spinal cord of an infected rabbit.

Nowadays, if you suspect that you have been exposed to rabies, you will be given a course of post-exposure prophylaxis or PEP. This consists of one dose of immune globulin and five doses of rabies vaccine over a 28-day period.

Treatment is relatively painless and is given in your arm, like a flu or tetanus vaccine.

REITER'S SYNDROME

What is it?
A type of reactive arthritis that is caused by a bacterial infection, named after Hans Reiter, who was the first to identify and treat this disease during the First World War.

Where can I catch it?
The bacteria that cause Reiter's syndrome are the same bacteria as can also cause food poisoning or chlamydia. Close contact with infected people, objects or surfaces can result in infection, and it can be sexually transmitted. After you have been ill with these types of bacterial infections, Reiter's syndrome may be triggered, as the bacteria can travel to other parts of your body, for example the joints, skin, eyes or muscles.

Major outbreaks
Reiter's syndrome appears internationally, most commonly in men between the ages of 20 to 40 years, three and one half of every 100,000 men under 50 annually. Women develop Reiter's syndrome less often.

How do I know I have it?
The syndrome affects several different parts of the body. Men may feel the need to urinate more often, and it will burn when urinating. You may have a penile discharge. Women can also feel burning when urinating, and can experience inflammation of the fallopian tubes, vulva, vagina, cervix or urethra.

Reiter's syndrome will give you arthritis, especially in your knees, ankles and feet, which will become swollen and painful. You may also develop spondylitis, or inflammation of the vertebrae in your spinal column.

Reiter's syndrome can also affect your eyes, causing an inflammation of the membrane that covers your eyeball (conjunctivitis) or of the inner eye (uveitis). If you develop these conditions, you will have red eyes that will feel sore and irritated, and your vision will be blurred.

It can affect your skin, giving you painless sores on the end of your penis, or rashes of hard bumps on the soles of your feet. You may also have recurring mouth ulcers.

Chances of survival
In rare cases, Reiter's syndrome can be fatal, usually as a result of adverse reactions to the treatment. It is most common in patients who are HIV

positive, so that HIV tests are offered following diagnosis. About 10 percent of patients with Reiter's syndrome will develop heart problems as a result of the disease.

How do I get rid of it?

There is no specific cure for Reiter's syndrome, but you will be offered treatment that can alleviate the symptoms. Bed rest can ease pressure on arthritic joints. Exercise helps improve your joints, especially exercises designed to strengthen the muscles around the joints. Anti-inflammatory drugs, including non-prescription aspirin and ibuprofen, are useful in combating inflammation and pain. For more severe inflammation, you may be given injections of corticosteroids. Skin lesions may be given corticosteroid creams, and antibiotics will help fight the bacterial infection that first caused the Reiter's syndrome to develop. In most cases, patients make a full recovery within six months of the first flare up of symptoms. About 20 percent of people will go on to have mild chronic arthritis and a much smaller percentage will have chronic severe and deforming arthritis.

RESPIRATORY SYNCYTIAL VIRUS (RSV)

What is it?
A common virus affecting the lungs.

Where can I catch it?
The virus passes from person to person in nasal fluid and oral fluid, entering the body when the eyes, nose or mouth are touched. It is the most common cause of respiratory infection in children.

Major outbreaks
Most children will have had an RSV infection by the age of two years. Once you have had the virus, you will develop some immunity, but will contract milder doses of the virus several times throughout your lifetime.

How do I know I have it?
In most young children the virus usually causes a heavy cold, with a fever, a cough (that can sound like a whooping cough, especially in babies), a runny nose and sometimes an ear infection. In older children and adults the virus usually affects the upper respiratory tract, causing infections of the throat, nose and sinuses.

Chances of survival
A first RSV infection can be more severe, and in infants under six months of age, it can also be fatal. There are about 90,000 people hospitalised with RSV infections every year, mostly children, due to severe breathing problems that need to be managed in the hospital. Every year approximately 4,500 children under the age of five years die from RSV. In those with underlying respiratory conditions or weak immune systems, the virus may progress to cause pneumonia.

How do I get rid of it?
A severe case of RSV may be treated with an anti-viral drug, such as Ribavarin, which needs to be inhaled; therefore it is given in a mist or oxygen tent. Some patients may also need mechanical assistance with their breathing, with a ventilator. Milder cases of the infection will clear without treatment.

What is it?

A serious inflammatory disease that can affect many parts of the body, including the heart, nervous system, joints and skin. A small percentage of people who have a strep throat (streptococcal) infection that is untreated will develop rheumatic fever a few weeks later.

Where can I catch it?

Anyone can catch it, but it most frequently occurs in children between six and 15 years old, and girls are twice as likely to get it as boys.

Major outbreaks

It is common in developing countries and much less common in developed countries because of the widespread use of antibiotics. Until 1960 it was the leading cause of death in children and a common cause of heart disease.

How do I know I have it?

Symptoms typically appear within a month of an untreated strep throat infection and include painful, swollen joints; tiredness and breathing difficulties; fever; abnormal heartbeat; involuntary jerking movements of the limbs and face, also known as St. Vitus' Dance (if the brain has become infected); a broad, pink, non-itching rash and, in rare cases, lumps under the skin.

Chances of survival

About half of those infected develop heart inflammation, but this doesn't always lead to permanent heart damage. In a small number of cases, the heart valves will be permanently scarred and surgery may be necessary to replace or repair them.

How do I get rid of it?

Three quarters of people recover within six weeks and fewer than five percent of people still have symptoms after six months. Early intervention with antibiotics and anti-inflammatory drugs is vital to kill the strep bacteria and limit damage to the heart valves. Often a follow-up course of antibiotics will last for several years to prevent further attacks.

RIFT VALLEY FEVER

What is it?
A viral disease caused by a Phlebovirus that can affect livestock and humans, first identified by veterinarians in Kenya in the early 20th century.

Where can I catch it?
Humans can catch Rift Valley fever if they are bitten by a mosquito that has become infected by livestock, or if they come into direct contact with body fluids of an infected animal, during the slaughtering process or by handling infected meat. There have also been cases where the virus has been contracted via inhalation in a laboratory holding specimens of the Rift Valley fever virus. It is found in cattle-rearing areas of southern and eastern Africa and Madagascar, although it is also present in most parts of sub-Saharan Africa. In 2000 the first cases outside Africa were identified in Saudi Arabia and Yemen.

Major outbreaks
There have been several large outbreaks of the virus in livestock, which have then spread to humans in recent years: in 1977 in Egypt, in 1987 in Senegal and from 1997 to 1998 in Kenya and Somalia. Most epidemics occur during periods of unusually heavy rainfall.

How do I know I have it?
You will show flu-like symptoms, feeling weak and lethargic, with backache, light-headedness and weight loss, lasting for up to a week.

Chances of survival
There is a one percent death rate for Rift Valley fever, and most fatalities are malnourished or live far from medical attention. Up to 10 percent of cases are left with vision problems or partial blindness, as the virus can cause an inflammation of the retina. The infection can also cause encephalitis (swelling of the brain) and hemorrhage (severe bleeding).

How do I get rid of it?
As yet there is no standard treatment for Rift Valley fever, but the anti-viral drug Ribavarin is currently being studied in connection with the virus in humans. There are also studies into a possible vaccine.

What is it?

A potentially serious disease caused by the bacterium *Rickettsia rickettsii*, named after Howard T. Ricketts, who first identified the bacteria. It was first known as 'Black Measles'.

Where can I catch it?

The bacterium that causes Rocky Mountain spotted fever is carried by ticks that most commonly live in the southeastern states of the United States, although there have been cases in nearly every state.

Major outbreaks

Rocky Mountain spotted fever is found in every state in the United States, with the exception of Hawaii, Vermont, Maine and Alaska. The majority of the 800 cases annually are reported between April and September, which is the most active season for ticks.

How do I know I have it?

You will have a very high temperature, often as high as 40ºC (104ºF), which will develop suddenly and can last for as long as three weeks. You will also have a bad headache, feel lethargic and listless, with chills, aching or painful muscles that feel very tender when touched, and nausea. Usually three to five days after the fever and headache begin, your rash will appear. Small red spots will cover your feet, wrists and hands and will then spread up your arms and legs, finally covering your trunk. After a few days, the spots may develop into bruises or blood spots under the skin.

Chances of survival

Without treatment Rocky Mountain spotted fever would kill up to 30 percent of those infected with the disease. It can cause damage to the heart, liver, kidneys and lungs. With treatment, mortality rates fall to four percent. In 25 percent of cases, patients become confused and lethargic, which can become more severe, leading to delirium, seizures and coma.

How do I get rid of it?

Rocky Mountain spotted fever is treated with antibiotics at home in milder cases or intravenously in the hospital in more severe cases.

ROTAVIRUS

What is it?
A viral infection of the digestive tract that gets its name from its wheel-shaped appearance under an electron microscope.

Where can I catch it?
Rotavirus is very easily spread from hand to mouth following contact with the stool of an infected person. It is most common in infants and children, particularly because children often forget to wash their hands properly after using the toilet or before eating.

Major outbreaks
Rotavirus is the most common cause of diarrhea in children, and it is estimated that it kills as many as 10 million people a year worldwide, with more than 600,000 of these being children.

How do I know I have it?
You will develop a fever and abdominal pain, and you will vomit and have watery diarrhea for up to nine days.

Chances of survival
The most serious complication is dehydration. Most children will recover without the need for medical intervention.

How do I get rid of it?
The virus should generally be allowed to run its course, with infected children and adults eating small amounts of food at regular intervals and drinking plenty of clear fluids. Fruit juices and other soft drinks can make the diarrhea worse. Where diarrhea is more severe, you may be given oral rehydration fluids. Eating live yogurts and foods containing the beneficial bacteria, Lactobacilllus, can help prevent rotavirus infection and can help minimise its effects.

What is it?
A bacterial infection caused by the Λ beta-hemolytic streptococcal bacteria.

Where can I catch it?
The bacteria is carried in the fluids of the nose and mouth, so you can become infected following close personal contact, by touching your eyes, nose or mouth after touching a surface or object infected with the bacteria, or sharing eating utensils with an infected person.

Major outbreaks
Outbreaks are most commonly seen in crowded environments, such as schools, with most cases occurring in the four- to eight-year-old age group. Approximately 80 percent of children have developed lifelong immunity to scarlet fever by the age of 10 years.

How do I know I have it?
Your throat will be red and very sore, the glands in your neck are likely to be swollen and you will have a temperature of over 38°C (100°F), probably with

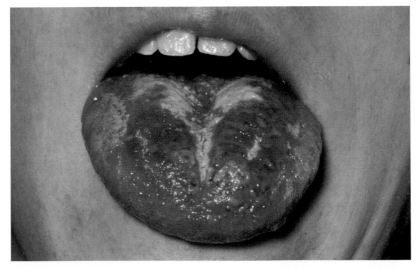

chills. About 12 hours after first showing these symptoms, a rash will appear on your trunk and may spread quickly all over your body. It looks like sunburn and feels rough, like sandpaper. Your face will be very red, and your tongue will have a thick white coating, with large, red, 'strawberry-like' bumps over it.

Chances of survival

Most cases of scarlet fever, if treated, will result in full recovery. However, complications do occur, including pneumonia, meningitis, brain abscesses and septicemia and can leave patients with heart or kidney damage that will require long-term treatment. The most serious complication of scarlet fever is streptococcal toxic shock syndrome, which is lethal.

How do I get rid of it?

Treating cases of 'Strep throat' infections early with antibiotics will prevent scarlet fever developing. If you have developed scarlet fever, you will be given the antibiotics penicillin or erythromycin. Warm liquids and cold foods will be the most soothing for your sore throat, and a cool mist humidifier will also help to ease the throat.

What is it?

A disease caused by schistosomes (parasitic worms), of which there are five species that affect humans: *schistosoma hematobium, S. intercalatum, S. japonicum, S. mansoni and S. mekongi*. These worms, which are carried in freshwater snails, were discovered in 1851 by a pathologist called Theodor Bilharz, after whom the disease is named.

Where can I catch it?

Water becomes contaminated by schistosoma eggs when infected people excrete into it. The eggs hatch, and the worms enter the freshwater snails where they develop. Then they leave the snail and re-enter the water, where they can infect human swimmers by penetrating the skin. They grow inside the blood vessels of their human hosts and produce eggs, some of which are excreted by the host, and the cycle begins again. The eggs that remain in the body build up and cause damage to the tissues of the intestines, bladder and other organs.

Major outbreaks

It is found mainly in tropical and subtropical regions such as South and Central America, Africa, Asia and Southeast Asia. There are an estimated 200 million people infected worldwide and three times as many people at risk of infection. It is estimated that 85 percent of all cases are in sub-Saharan Africa.

How do I know I have it?

A few days after becoming infected you may develop a rash or itchy tingling skin (also known as 'swimmer's itch'). A few months later you may develop a fever, muscle aches, enlarged glands, diarrhea and a cough, but many people show no symptoms early on. As the eggs continue to build up in your body tissues, you will feel increasingly unwell. In rare cases the eggs end up in the brain or spinal cord and can cause seizures or even paralysis.

Chances of survival

Repeated and prolonged infection will cause death by damaging your internal organs, but it is difficult to estimate how many people die from this infection because the complications that lead to death will often disguise a diagnosis of schistosomiasis.

How do I get rid of it?

Thirty years ago the treatment was as dangerous as the disease, but now modern drugs such as Praziquantel, Oxamniquine and Metrifonate can be used safely with few side effects.

What is it?

A viral infection of the respiratory tract commonly known as SARS, caused by the SARS-associated coronavirus, or SARS-CoV, which was first reported in Southern China in November 2002.

Where can I catch it?

Close contacted with a person infected with the SARS-CoV virus is the easiest way to catch SARS. The virus becomes airborne when an infected person sneezes or coughs, and can be propelled across distances of about 90 centimetres in this way. It can also be deposited on surfaces or objects after a cough or a sneeze and will transfer to your eyes, nose or mouth by touch. Any of the following activities with an infected person will put you at risk of developing the virus: kissing, close conversation or sharing cutlery or drinking vessels.

Major outbreaks

The outbreak of SARS that took place worldwide from November 2002 to July 2003 affected more than 8,000 people. Those infected were predominantly from China and Hong Kong, with cases also reported in Taiwan, Canada, Singapore, Vietnam, Malaysia, the Philippines, Thailand, South Africa and the United States. Outside China and Hong Kong, outbreaks began with a first victim who had contracted the virus during a visit to an infected area. There are currently no known cases of SARS anywhere in the world.

How do I know I have it?

You will develop a temperature above 38°C (100°F), and may also have a headache, muscle aches, chills and a cough. You may begin to feel dizzy and develop diarrhea. In most cases, the disease progresses to become pneumonia.

Chances of survival

The WHO has calculated that mortality rates during the 2003 outbreak averaged 15 percent. Mortality rates are higher amongst older populations, reaching as much as 56.8 percent for those over 64 years.

How do I get rid of it?

Treatment will vary, as there is no specific recognised protocol, but you are likely to be treated with broad-spectrum antibiotics and the anti-viral drugs Ribavarin and Kaletra. Depending on the severity of the case, you may also be given steroids to help repair any damage to your lungs, and your breathing may be given assistance in the form of either intubation or a mechanical ventilator.

What is it?

An infectious disease caused by the *Shigella* family of bacteria, which was discovered by a Japanese scientist called Shiga in 1897, who named it after himself. The bacteria infect the intestinal tract.

Where can I catch it?

The bacteria are present in the stools of infected people, and most cases are passed on by contact with the stools, through poor hygiene (not washing hands after going to the bathroom). It is common among toddlers who are likely to put their fingers in their mouth. It can also be passed from the hands or by insects such as flies onto food. Water can become contaminated if sewage is allowed to run into it.

Major outbreaks

In the developing world, shigellosis is very common, and about 18,000 cases of shigellosis are reported each year in the United States, where it is more prevalent in summer than winter. Many cases are undetected because they are so mild, so the actual number of infections may be as many as 400,000.

How do I know I have it?

One or two days after becoming infected you will develop diarrhea, fever and stomach cramps. Your stools may contain blood and mucus. You may show no symptoms at all, but can still pass it to others if you don't wash your hands after visiting the bathroom.

About three percent of those infected with *Shigella flexneri* develop Reiter's syndrome, with joint pains, irritation of the eyes and painful urination.

Chances of survival

The elderly and young children may need hospitalisation if the symptoms are particularly severe, but shigellosis should resolve itself within a week, although in some cases it may be several months before your bowel movements return to normal.

How do I get rid of it?

Some shigella bacteria are resistant to antibiotics, but most cases can be treated with ampicillin, trimethoprim/ sulfamethoxazole, nalidixic acid or ciprofloxacin.

SHINGLES

What is it?

Also known as herpes zoster, it is caused by the dormant chicken-pox virus reappearing to cause illness in the body of a person who has already had chicken pox.

Where can I catch it?

Once a person has contracted chicken pox, the virus migrates to the nerve roots, where it lies dormant for many years until an unknown trigger causes it to re-emerge and travel back to the skin. Seventy percent of cases occur in people over 50 years old, and the risk increases the older you get (one study estimated that an 85 year old has a 50 percent chance of having shingles).

You cannot 'catch' shingles from someone else, since it is a second outbreak of a virus that is already in your body from an earlier infection. However, a person with shingles can pass on chicken pox to someone who hasn't already had it.

Major outbreaks

Millions are affected worldwide each year, and there are about 800,000 cases in the United States each year. More than one in 10 people who contracted chickenpox in childhood will develop shingles.

How do I know I have it?

It causes numbness and itching and shooting pains that last for several weeks or even months (known as postherpetic neuralgia). A few days later a blister-like rash appears on one side of your body, and this is often accompanied by a fever, headache and enlarged lymph nodes. The blisters burst, scab over after three to five days and fall off a few weeks later.

Chances of survival

Shingles is rarely fatal to those with healthy immune systems, but the nerve damage and associated pain can be prolonged and very unpleasant. If the rash appears on your face you should see an ophthalmologist, because it may cause blindness and other eye problems.

How do I get rid of it?

There is no cure, but antiviral agents (e.g. acyclovir) are sometimes given to older people, but they must be used during the first 72 hours. You can also try antihistamines to relieve the itching.

What is it?

Smallpox is a serious, contagious and sometimes fatal infectious disease caused by the variola virus. Historically known as 'the pox', which refers to the raised bumps that appear on the face and body of an infected person.

There are two clinical forms: variola major is the severe and most common form of smallpox with a 30 percent fatality rate, and variola minor is the other and is much less severe and has only a one percent fatality rate.

Where can I catch it?

Smallpox has been eliminated, so the only place you're going to catch it is from bioterrorism or if you're a scientist working with the virus.

Generally, you need direct and fairly prolonged face-to-face contact with an infected human (animals and insects are not known to be carriers), their body fluids or contaminated clothes or bedding.

Major outbreaks

Smallpox is believed to have originated over 3,000 years ago. In earlier years, epidemics swept across continents killing large populations, attacking royalty and peasants alike, killing 30 percent of those infected and leaving survivors with scars and sometimes blind.

The disease was finally eradicated by 1977 after a decade of vaccinations worldwide.

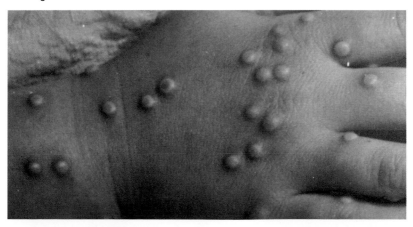

How do I know I have it?

After exposure to the virus you'll feel
fine for up to two weeks, until the first
symptoms appear: high fever, fatigue,
head and body aches and sometimes
vomiting. Then two to four days later
you'll develop small red spots on your
tongue and in your mouth, which will
develop into open sores, followed by
first facial and then a body rash as the
fever subsides. The rash will turn into
raised bumps filled with thick puss, and
you will once again be gripped by fever
until the bumps harden and form scabs.
When the scabs eventually drop off
you'll be left with pitted scars, but at
least you'll no longer be contagious.

Chances of survival

With modern treatment, very good.

How do I get rid of it?

Once you've got it, you're stuck with
it. There is no specific treatment for
smallpox disease, and the only
prevention is vaccination.

What is it?
A parasitic infection of the intestines caused by the roundworm, *Strongyloides stercoralis*.

Where can I catch it?
Strongyloides can penetrate your skin if you come into contact with infected soil. Once it is in your body, it travels up to the lungs, through to the back of your mouth, where it is swallowed and matures in your intestines. There it will lay eggs that pass in the stool, where it can re-infect the carrier, causing infections lasting many years.

Major outbreaks
The roundworm is most endemic in the warm, moist areas of the tropics, especially in Africa, particularly the Sudan, Kenya and Ethiopia. It is also found in the southern United States.

How do I know I have it?
Often people infected with strongyloides will have no symptoms at all. Where infections do have symptoms, you may complain of abdominal pain, diarrhea, a skin rash resembling hives around the anus, a cough, weight loss, nausea and vomiting.

Chances of survival
Most otherwise healthy people who become infected with the strongyloides roundworm will have a mild infection lasting over a long time period, and such infestations are rarely fatal. However, strongyloidiasis can be severe, especially in the case of 'hyperinfection syndrome' and 'disseminated strongyloidiasis'. This is where the normal life cycle of the roundworm becomes accelerated so that many worms develop very quickly, or where the infestation spreads to organs of the body outside of the intestine. These forms of the disease have high fatalities, as high as 80 percent, and are usually seen in patients whose immune systems are already compromised due to other underlying conditions.

How do I get rid of it?
Strongyloidiasis is treated with one of several anti-worm drugs, such as Albendazole, Ivermectin or Thiabendazole.

SYPHILIS

What is it?
A STD caused by the bacterium *Treponema pallidum*.

Where can I catch it?
You must come into contract with the syphilitic sore of someone suffering from the disease, usually through vaginal, anal or oral sex. These sores are usually on the external genitals, vagina, anus or in the rectum, but they also occur on the lips and mouth, so even kissing can spread the infection, but it cannot be caught from toilet seats, doorknobs or swimming pools.

Major outbreaks
There are about 12 million people infected worldwide. About 70,000 cases are reported in the United States each year, and most of these occur in people between 20 to 39 years of age.

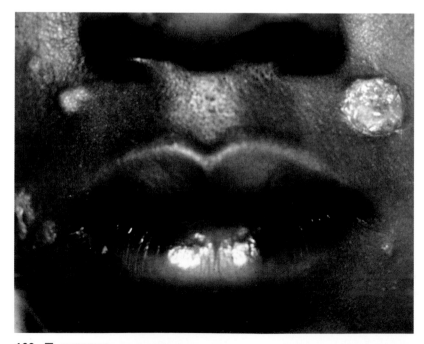

How do I know I have it?

There are four stages of the disease. Between 10 days to three months after infection, during the primary stage, you will develop a single firm, round, small, painless sore (a chancre) at the point where the infection entered your body (although you may then develop many sores). The sore lasts for about three to six weeks. Without treatment you enter the second stage and develop a rash of reddish-brown spots on your palms and bottoms of your feet. You may also have swollen lymph glands, sore throat, patchy hair loss, headaches, weight loss, muscle aches and fatigue. When these symptoms disappear you have entered the latent stage, with no further symptoms, while serious internal damage is taking place so that years later, by the final stage, you may have poor co-ordination, paralysis, heart problems, blindness and dementia. Untreated it can be fatal. A blood test can confirm whether you are infected.

Chances of survival

Without treatment the serious internal damage that occurs during the final stages of the disease causes serious disability and death.

How do I get rid of it?

In its early stages a simple shot of penicillin will cure you or a course of antibiotics during the later stages.

TAENIASIS
(Tapeworm)

What is it?
A tapeworm infestation of the digestive tract.

Where can I catch it?
Taeniasis is caused by eating the raw or undercooked meat from infected pigs, cows, freshwater fish and salmon.

Major outbreaks
Tapeworm infestations in humans occur worldwide, but are especially common in areas where the soil or water supply is contaminated by feces, and where the local population consumes raw or lightly cooked meat and fish. Infestations are common in Latin America, parts of Africa, the Middle East and Central Asia.

How do I know I have it?

In most cases, people who have a tapeworm infestation will not be aware of it, as they are not likely to have any symptoms except for noticing moving sections of the tapeworm passing in their stools. Children may have diarrhea, fatigue and complain of stomach pain.

Chances of survival

Taeniasis is rarely fatal, but it can cause serious complications. Larval cysts can travel to other parts of the body from the stomach; in the eye this can result in a detached retina and in the brain or spinal cord, this can cause headaches, seizures, loss of balance or a swelling of the brain.

How do I get rid of it?

You will be given an anti-parasitic drug, usually orally in a single dose, most commonly Niclosamide. Cysts in the eye may not respond to the drug and may have to be removed surgically.

TETANUS

What is it?

A disease of the nervous system caused by *Clostridium tetani* bacteria, which are present worldwide, especially in soil, dust and manure. Also known as 'lockjaw'.

Where can I catch it?

The spores of the bacteria enter the body through a break in the skin, which may be anything from a small scratch to a large wound. People are commonly infected from animal bites, splinters, rusty nails or getting dirt in a cut. You cannot 'catch' tetanus from another person.

Major outbreaks

While tetanus can occur anywhere in the world, neonatal (newborn) tetanus is very common in developing countries

and causes more than 270,000 deaths worldwide per year. This occurs when the umbilical cord is cut in non-sterile conditions, or becomes infected. In many cultures a substance such as ash, oil or butter, and, in some cases, mud and animal dung are applied to the stump, thus hugely increasing the risk of tetanus infection.

How do I know I have it?

The bacteria act on the central nervous system. Symptoms usually appear about a week after infection. These include a headache and stiffness in the jaw, followed by a stiff neck, difficulty swallowing, stomach stiffness and later, elevated blood pressure, severe muscle spasms and fever. The convulsions are so severe that you risk breaking your spine, or other bones.

Chances of survival

About 10 percent of infected people die; of those, many are over 60 years of age.

How do I get rid of it?

While there is no 'cure', you should receive hospital treatment to manage and monitor your symptoms. The best prevention is vaccination. Even people who have just recovered from a tetanus infection are not immune without vaccination.

What is it?

When we say that a dog or cat has worms, we are usually referring to the round-worms *Toxocara canis* and *Toxocara cati*. In humans, toxocariasis is caused by swallowing the eggs of this parasite, found in the feces of infected dogs and cats.

Where can I catch it?

Infection occurs anywhere that infected feces are present, often in the soil of parks and playgrounds and homes where dogs and cats are pets. Toxocara eggs can survive for years in the environment. Once the eggs reach the intestine, they hatch into larvae that penetrate the bowel wall and travel through the body.

Major outbreaks

Toxocariasis is found worldwide and is common in children, because they are more likely to become infected through playing in infected soil or sandpits and then putting their fingers in their mouths. More than 1,000 people each year experience permanent vision loss as a result.

How do I know I have it?

There are three basic forms of the infection. The first causes a mild fever, cough, abdominal pain, headaches and behavioural problems. The second, *visceral larva migrans*, occurs with heavy or repeated infection causing swelling of organs, fever, coughing, asthma and pneumonia when the larvae travel through the body, causing a range of problems and, in extreme cases, myocarditis or respiratory failure. The third, *Ocular larva migrans*, is caused by larvae entering the back of the eye, causing impaired vision and possible blindness. If the brain becomes infected, the victim will suffer seizures.

Chances of survival

Most cases are not serious, and many people show no symptoms. With treatment the outcome is good, except in cases of eye or brain infection. Liver or eye infection may require chemotherapy. Eye infection often requires laser surgery.

How do I get rid of it?

Treatment is with anti-parasitic and anti-inflammatory drugs. Proper hygiene is essential, washing hands after gardening or playing in sandpits or after contact with cats or dogs, and ensuring that pets are treated regularly for worms.

TOXOPLASMOSIS

What is it?

A parasitic infection caused by a one-celled parasite called *Toxoplasma gondii*.

Where can I catch it?

The parasites are most commonly found in cat feces and in the soil, so they can be picked up from gardening or emptying a cat's litter tray and then putting your fingers in your mouth before washing them. The cat is the only organism in which the parasite can reproduce. After a cat has excreted the parasites they can infect people for up to a week later. They are also found in raw meat (particularly pork, lamb and venison) and poorly washed vegetables and can infect drinking water.

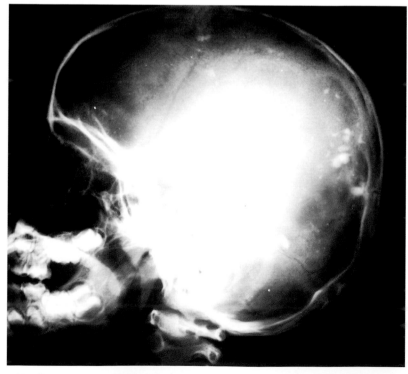

If a pregnant woman becomes infected she can pass it on to her unborn child, which may result in miscarriage or serious eye or brain damage at birth.

Major outbreaks
The disease is found worldwide, and in the United States it is estimated that 60 million people carry the parasite and have antibodies, many without symptoms.

How do I know I have it?
Most people don't realise they are infected, although a small number may experience mild flu-like symptoms aches and pains and enlarged glands. An even smaller number will develop severe headaches, weakness on one side of the body, fever, seizures and problems with eyesight and co-ordination.

Chances of survival
While the disease has serious consequences for those with weakened immune systems and pregnant women, the majority of people suffer no ill effects.

How do I get rid of it?
Mild cases do not require treatment, but a pregnant woman who discovers she has toxoplasmosis will be treated with a combination of an anti-malarial drug, pyrimethamine and the antibiotic sulfadiazole.

TRACHOMA
(Egyptian Ophthalmia, Granular Conjunctivitis)

What is it?
A chronic form of conjunctivitis caused by the bacterium *Chlamydia trachomatis*. It was first described in a 16th-century-BC Papyrus. It causes scarring of the cornea and thickening of the mucous membrane that lines the inner surface of the eyelid and the eyeball. The eyelid becomes distorted and the eyelashes often curl inwards to irritate the cornea, which eventually becomes opaque. It is the world's leading cause of preventable blindness. Children under the age of 10 are at risk of repeat infections.

Where can I catch it?
It occurs worldwide, especially in rural areas in developing countries. It affects over 400 million people (mainly in Africa, the Middle East and Asia). It is rare in the developed countries, although those beneath the poverty line and living in crowded, unsanitary conditions with poor healthcare are at greatly increased risk.

You catch it by coming into contact with secretions from an infected person's eye or nose and throat. These secretions can be transferred on inanimate objects such as clothes and bedding. Flies can also transmit the disease.

Major outbreaks
The WHO estimates that six million people become blind because of trachoma each year. In some African countries a staggering 40 percent of children are affected.

How do I know I have it?
Trachoma affects the inner upper eyelid and cornea, which become inflamed; your eyes will feel very uncomfortable, red and sore and weepy. You may also be light sensitive, and your eyelids will swell painfully. During the advanced stages of the disease, your upper eyelid will turn inwards and your cornea will be opaque and scarred.

Chances of survival
It is not life-threatening, and if treated early with antibiotics, you should make a full recovery. Without treatment you will lose your sight.

How do I get rid of it?
Take antibiotics such as tetracycline drugs or sulfonamides, erythromycin and its derivatives, or doxycycline. In some cases eyelid surgery may be necessary.

What is it?

It is a chronic bacterial infection and ulceration of the gums. It is a rare and severe form of gingivitis (gum inflammation) and is also known as acute necrotizing ulcerative gingivitis, or Vincent's stomatitis.

Where can I catch it?

The mouth contains a balance of 'good' and 'bad' bacteria. Trench mouth develops when this balance is disrupted, causing infection and ulcers. It is caused by poor oral hygiene, poor nutrition, stress and smoking. People with compromised immune systems are at greatest risk, such as those with HIV/AIDS (see page 60).

Major outbreaks

It occurs anywhere that poor oral hygiene is practised or the immune system is weakened. It most often affects adults under 35 years of age.

How do I know I have it?

Symptoms may appear suddenly. Gums are painful, bleed easily and profusely and are red and swollen. There are ulcers between the teeth. You will have bad breath and a foul taste in your mouth. The gums may be grey where tissue has died and rotted. In some cases the lymph nodes in the head and neck may become swollen.

Chances of survival

Without treatment the infection may spread to cheeks, lips and jaw and may result in the loss of teeth. Occasionally the infection spreads to the bloodstream and is life-threatening.

How do I get rid of it?

Good oral hygiene and nutrition are essential. Brush after every meal and at bedtime and floss regularly. Saltwater rinses may be used to soothe gums, and hydrogen peroxide may be recommended to remove dead gum tissue.

What is it?
A common STD caused by *Trichomonas vaginalis*, one of three single-celled parasites called trichomonads that infect humans. It affects both women and, to a lesser extent, men and is the most common curable STD.

Where can I catch it?
Vaginal sex is the most common way of becoming infected, but the parasite can also be spread on objects such as underwear, towels and sex toys. Non-sexual infection is rare.

It usually affects women, but men can catch it too, although they rarely experience any symptoms. The vagina is the most common place of infection in women and the urethra in men.

Major outbreaks
More than 200 million people are infected worldwide, and about two million new cases occur in the United States each year, especially in women between the ages of 16 and 35.

How do I know I have it?
Between five to 28 days after infection, many women experience a frothy green, yellow or grey vaginal discharge that is smelly, vaginal itching and pain during sex and when urinating. Most men don't have any symptoms, although some may feel a burning sensation inside their penis after urinating or ejaculating.

Chances of survival
The only danger of having the infection is increased susceptibility to HIV and, in women, an increased risk of inflammation of the fallopian tubes. Pregnant women with trichomoniasis may have premature babies with lower birth weights. Otherwise, the infection is not fatal or harmful.

How do I get rid of it?
The antibiotics tinidazole and metronidazole are effective. Although symptoms will usually disappear without treatment within a few weeks, it is important to get treatment to stop you from passing on the infection.

What is it?
A parasitic intestinal infection caused by the whipworm *Trichocephalus trichiura*. The adult worm grows up to five centimetres long and lives for three years.

Where can I catch it?
It is common worldwide, especially in countries with warm, humid climates. Whipworm eggs are found in the soil. It is one of the most common human parasites. Once the eggs have been swallowed, they hatch in the intestine, and a few weeks later, when they reach maturity, mating begins. A female worm can produce up to 20,000 eggs each day, which are passed in the stools ready to re-infect others.

Major outbreaks
There are an estimated 800 million infections worldwide, especially in areas with poor sanitation in tropical climates: Southeast Asia, Africa, the Caribbean and Central and South America, where up to 80 percent of people are infected.

How do I know I have it?
If you only ingest a few eggs, you will probably have no symptoms. Heavier infestations result in bloody diarrhea.

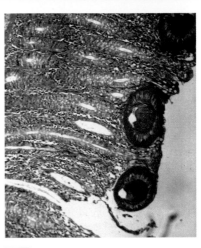

Chances of survival
It is only life-threatening in cases of long-standing infection, where blood loss may cause anemia, and severe dehydration associated with the diarrhea is dangerous if fluids are not replaced. Really nasty cases (infection with thousands of worms) result in rectal prolapse, which means that a lump of rectal tissue slides out of your anus.

How do I get rid of it?
Anti-parasitic drugs, such as mebendazole, are commonly used. With treatment, full recovery is expected.

TUBERCULOSIS
(TB, Consumption, Wasting Disease, White Plague)

What is it?
An ancient infectious disease that has been around for over 30,000 years. It is caused by infection from *Mycobacterium tuberculosis* bacteria, and most cases affect the lungs.

Where can I catch it?
It is found worldwide. The bacilli spores are transmitted through the air when an infected person coughs or sneezes, but you have to spend quite a long time with an infected person who has not been treated to catch TB. It cannot be transmitted by objects such as bed linen or clothes, although it is

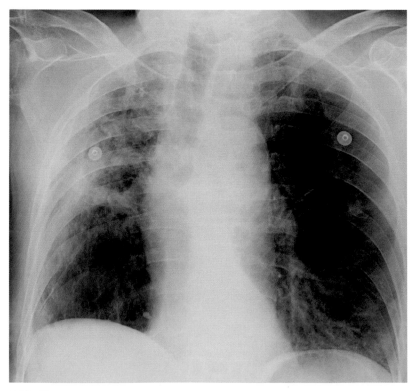

possible to contract TB by drinking unpasteurized milk products from an infected cow.

Major outbreaks

Nearly two million people worldwide die from TB each year, and a further two million are infected and risk developing the active form of the disease.

How do I know I have it?

There are two types of TB. The first is latent TB infection, which has no symptoms. Only 10 percent of those people go on to develop the second or active type of TB, although they remain infectious and can spread it to others. The only way to tell if you have latent TB infection is to take a skin test and a chest X-ray.

People with active TB have a bad cough (and may cough up blood), chest pain, weakness, weight loss, loss of appetite, fever and night sweats.

Chances of survival

TB used to be a slow death penalty, and still is in undeveloped countries where medication is in short supply. In the developed world, TB can be controlled with medication.

How do I get rid of it?

You must undergo a six-month course of drug treatment. Medication includes isoniazid and rifampin and a combination of other drugs. It is vital to complete the course, even though you may start to feel 'cured' within a couple of weeks; otherwise the TB will become resistant to the drugs, and you will suffer a relapse. Once you are being treated you are no longer contagious.

TULAREMIA
(Rabbit Fever)

What is it?
A highly infectious disease caused by the bacterium *Francisella tularensis*, found in animals, especially rodents, rabbits and hares.

Where can I catch it?
It occurs in the United States, Europe and Asia. You cannot catch it from another person, but it only takes a very small number of bacteria (as few as 10) to get tularemia, through an animal or insect bite (often a tick, mosquito or deerfly), handling animal carcasses, contaminated food, water or soil or breathing in the bacteria.

Major outbreaks
The largest modern outbreak occurred in Sweden in from 1966 to 1967 with 600 reported cases, most of whom were farm workers. A recent outbreak in Kosovo was a suspected case of bioterrorism, although it may have been linked to an increase in rodents due to unharvested crops. There are about 200 reported cases in the United States each year, and there were minor outbreaks in Martha's Vineyard in the 1970s. Rabbit hunters are at increased risk, hence the name rabbit fever.

Its potential as a dangerous biological weapon has been explored, and it was stockpiled by the superpowers after World War II. In 1970 a WHO expert committee predicted that if 50 kilograms of *F. tularensis* bacteria were spread over a city with a population of five million, it would result in 250,000 casualties and 19,000 deaths.

How do I know I have it?
Symptoms appear between three and 14 days after infection and include fever, headaches, diarrhea, chest pain, breathing problems, muscle aches, weakness, joint pain and a dry cough (you may cough up blood), skin or mouth ulcers, swollen eyes and a sore throat.

Chances of survival
The disease is fatal if you do not receive the correct antibiotics. Between five and 15 percent of those who catch the Type A strain of the disease have died. If you develop heart problems or blood poisoning and do not receive antibiotics, your chances of dying are as high as 30 to 60 percent.

How do I get rid of it?

It is vital you receive antibiotics including Aminoglycosides, macrolides, chloramphenicol and fluoroquinolones. A vaccine is currently under review by the United States Food and Drug Administration.

What is it?
An infestation of the skin with
the pregnant flea, *Tunga penetrans*,
commonly known as a chigger or jigger.
The infestation was first noted by the
crewmen sailing with Christopher
Columbus.

Where can I catch it?
Tungiasis is common throughout
Africa, the west coast of India and
Central and South America. The jigger,
or sand flea, lives in dusty or sandy soil,
and the adult female will penetrate the
skin when pregnant, usually on the
soles of your feet or the skin beside
your toenails if you walk barefoot in
infested areas.

Major outbreaks
The jigger flea is endemic in some areas,
where infection rates can be as high as
40 percent of the population.

How do I know I have it?
You will have one or two small, itchy
bumps or nodules, usually on your feet,
which will grow in size over the course
of eight to 12 days until they are pea-
sized. It has been known for a single
patient to have hundreds of nodules
at one time. The flea expels her eggs
through the centre of the nodule over
the next few weeks. The infestation can
ulcerate and become swollen.

Chances of survival
In the case of heavy infestations, or
where the flea dies in your skin, there
is a high risk that tungiasis can cause
secondary infections, such as gangrene,
which may result in the loss of a toe, or
tetanus, which can be fatal.

How do I get rid of it?
The jigger can be removed with forceps
after which the site should be cleaned
with alcohol to prevent further infection.

What is it?
A life-threatening contagious infection of the intestines caused by *Salmonella typhi* bacteria.

Where can I catch it?
If you eat food or drink water that has been contaminated by the stools or urine of an infected person, you will ingest the bacteria, which can survive for weeks in water or dried sewage. It can also be spread person to person by touching, if the infected person hasn't washed their hands. For this reason, typhoid is more common in countries with poor sanitation and poor access to clean drinking water, such as Asia, Africa and Latin America.

Major outbreaks
It affects about 12.5 million people worldwide each year. About 400 cases occur in the United States each year, usually in travellers.

How do I know I have it?
Once the bacteria have been swallowed, they multiply quickly in the gallbladder, bile ducts or liver and pass into the bowel. When it enters the bloodstream one to two weeks after infection, this will give you symptoms such as a high temperature (up to 40ºC/104ºF), sore throat, vomiting, chest congestion, diarrhea, skin rash and weakness, and the illness may last up to six weeks. A stool or blood culture is the only way to confirm that you have typhoid.

Chances of survival
Without treatment you will be sick for months, and 10 percent of people die from overwhelming infection and complications such as pneumonia and intestinal bleeding. With treatment you should make a full recovery.

How do I get rid of it?
Typhoid fever can be treated with antibiotics such as trimethoprim-sulfamethoxazole and ciprofloxacin, which will improve your symptoms within a few days. You should wash your hands scrupulously after visiting the bathroom and have another stool culture after treatment to confirm that you are no longer a carrier.

What is it?
A mosquito-borne flavivirus that affects the central nervous system. It was discovered in the West Nile District of Uganda in 1937. Mosquitoes become infected when they feed on infected birds and then pass it on to humans.

Where can I catch it?
It is found in Africa, West Asia and the Middle East, and it appeared in the United States in 1999. It is related to the St. Louis encephalitis virus also found in the United States. The most common cause of infection is from a mosquito bite, although it has also been spread through blood transfusions and breast-feeding. You can't get it through touching or kissing a person with the virus, and it cannot spread directly from birds, although you should still avoid handling dead birds.

Major outbreaks
In 1974 an epidemic in South Africa affected 3,000 people, and in Romania from 1996 to 1997, an outbreak of 500 cases resulted in over 50 deaths. It is not known how many people are affected worldwide. It is a growing problem in the United States. In 2003 there were 9,862 cases in the United States and 264 deaths.

How do I know I have it?
Most people show no symptoms and never know they have the virus, or suffer the mildest of flu-like symptoms (fever, headache and muscle aches) between three to 14 days after becoming infected. Less than one percent of those infected (most of whom are over 50 years of age) develop meningitis or encephalitis and require hospitalisation.

Chances of survival
Mild symptoms don't need any medical intervention, but if you develop severe symptoms, you will need hospital treatment to treat the complications (although there is no treatment against the virus itself). Death rates range between three to 15 percent, and most of these are elderly.

How do I get rid of it?
There is no treatment against the virus and there is no human vaccine.

What is it?
A harmless growth of tissue on the upper or lower eyelids.

Major outbreaks
Although the condition is seen internationally, it is very rare.

Where can I catch it?
The precise cause of xanthelasma is not known, but it generally appears in people over the age of 40 in both sexes and in all races. It can often indicate high cholesterol levels, especially in people below the age of 40 years.

How do I know I have it?
You will have soft, yellowish spots on your eyelids, probably your upper lid, which are oval in shape and are often symmetrical. They are not painful.

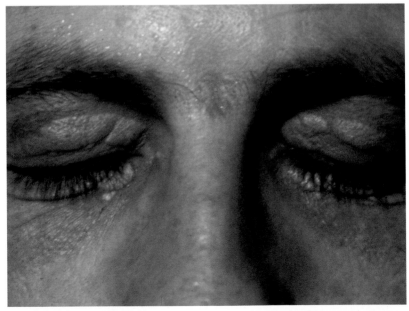

Chances of survival

The growths are not cancerous,
nor precancerous. If the xanthelasma
is caused by increased cholesterol,
however, you will be at a greater risk
of developing heart disease.

How do I get rid of it?

Some growths will disappear on
their own, but in other cases, multiple
xanthelasmas may merge together, or
coalesce, and become permanent. They
can be removed surgically, whereby the
growths are frozen with liquid nitrogen
that kills the fatty tissue. However they
will often recur. If your cholesterol is
high, you will be recommended to
improve your diet and fitness, and may
also be prescribed drugs to help bring
down levels of lipids (fats) in your
blood, such as Mevacor, Prevachol
or Zocor.

What is it?
A virus carried by the mosquitoes, especially *Aedes aegypti*, causing potentially life-threatening illness.

Where can I catch it?
The mosquitoes that carry yellow fever are only found in parts of tropical South America and sub-Saharan Africa. Jungle yellow fever is passed to humans in tropical rain forests, when they are bitten by a mosquito that has become infected with the virus after biting an infected monkey. Urban yellow fever passes from person to person by mosquito bites.

Major outbreaks
The disease is most prevalent in sub-Saharan Africa, where it is endemic, and affects over 30 countries with a total population of over 460 million people. yellow fever is also endemic in Bolivia, Brazil, Columbia, Ecuador and Peru. Despite a safe and effective vaccination that has been available for 60 years, there are now large proportions of the populations in vulnerable areas that have not been immunised, making yellow fever a serious public health issue. Dense urban populations of the mosquito, *Aedes aegypti*, make the risk of epidemics very high.

How do I know I have it?
Milder cases of yellow fever will leave you with flu-like symptoms, including fever, backache, headache, nausea and loss of appetite. You may vomit and your pulse may slow, but after four days or so, your symptoms should disappear. But in 15 percent of cases, yellow fever will progress to a second stage, known as the 'toxic phase'. Your fever will come back, and you will become jaundiced, have a painful abdomen and vomit blood from the stomach. Your mouth, nose and eyes may also bleed. Your kidneys will be badly affected, and you may stop urinating (kidney failure).

Chances of survival
The toxic phase of yellow fever has a 50 percent fatality rate. There is generally no major organ damage in the remainder of cases.

How do I get rid of it?
As there is no specific treatment for yellow fever, you will be given bed rest and plenty of fluids. It is important to keep yourself protected from mosquitoes during your infection so as to prevent the spread of the virus to others.

What is it?
A rare condition where tumors form in the pancreas and duodenum and the stomach becomes ulcerated.

Where can I catch it?
The causes of Zollinger-Ellison syndrome are not known. It develops at an average age of 50 years.

Major outbreaks
Zollinger-Ellison syndrome is very rare, affecting an estimated three in every one million Americans, with similar figures in Sweden and less than 0.5 cases per million in Ireland and Denmark. It occurs internationally and affects all races.

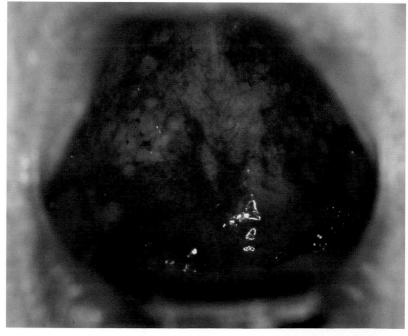

How do I know I have it?

You will have an upper abdominal pain that feels like a burning or gnawing. You will feel nauseous and have sickness and diarrhea. You will lose weight and feel tired. Your symptoms will be severe, and will not be relieved with over-the-counter antacids. Your stools may contain yellow fat and you may have gastrointestinal bleeding. In order to confirm that you have this condition, you will undergo a procedure called an upper gastrointestinal endoscopy, whereby a thin flexible camera is passed into your stomach via your throat and a small tissue sample is taken.

Chances of survival

Death rates from Zollinger-Ellison syndrome have fallen because of better surgical intervention, but 50 percent of the tumors are malignant, which means they become cancerous and can then spread to your liver and your lymph nodes.

How do I get rid of it?

You may have to undergo surgery to have the tumor(s) removed, but if the tumors are small and/or numerous, you may be given drugs to reduce the acid content in your stomach. The doctors may attempt to destroy the tumor by cutting off its blood supply (embolization) or by blasting it with an electrical current (radio-frequency ablation). Malignant tumors may also be treated with anti-cancer drugs (chemo-therapy). If you develop a severe form of the condition, your entire stomach may need to be surgically removed, though this is a rare procedure today. Once your tumors have been treated, you will be given medication to help control your ulcers, for example proton pump inhibitors or acid blockers, both of which reduce the amount of acid produced, which reduces pain and helps the ulcers heal.